UNLEASH YOUR
CAREER POTENTIAL

Advance Praise

"Completely inspiring. A work that shows the most critical career human side. Recounts the challenges, experiences, and ups and downs that many of us face in our work environments. Challenges the status quo, extols the potential of human talent, and motivates us to introspect on our values, objectives, and strengths. The book becomes an extraordinary tool to assimilate the challenges posed by an increasingly globalized and digital transformation that we are living right now."

–**Mauricio Monge Quesada**, Editor in Chief, Markets & Trends Central America, communication strategist with more than eight years in publishing, media and project leadership

"This book offers you a practical and deep path to connect your personal purpose to your career. A powerful key that will allow you not only leverage your career but mainly collaborate with the change you want to see in the world. What a guide!"

–**Fernanda Sato**, Corporate Change Maker and Women in STEM Lead, Brazil

"More than a truly great book; captivating, insightful, brilliant. Breaks the mold by not only providing examples but also giving a practical guide, step by step for each of the readers to become CEOs of their careers."

–**Timothy Scott Hall**, Global Transnational leader in Latin America

Unleash Your Career Potential is an inspiring book, containing a provocative call to action. Seven steps guide us through the book–relating experiences with practical exercises–to help us become aware of our level of job satisfaction, our expectations, dreams, values, and, above all, give us a roadmap to take action and achieve that professional career dream. Unquestionably, taking out a notebook and colored pencils, as requested by the author, will be a fascinating experience for the reader who dares to take on the challenge of not only reading this book, but also acting in accordance."

–**Martha Castillo**, Economist, Director
of Deloitte Academy Costa Rica

"Karla is a role model, change agent, and leader. This book is showing women and men what is truly possible when they step into their greatness and become the CEO of their career and life. This book is a gift for anyone that wants to live their full potential."

–**Michelle de Matheu**, aka The Soul Stylist,
Spiritual life and Business coach, USA

"This *Unleash Your Career Potential* book is a life changing book. The author, Karla, used her own professional career experiences and examples to guide people step by step through how to achieve a meaningful career that's full of fulfillment. Karla focused on how we can be the best version of ourselves and bring the most value to people. This book is a best book ever."

–**Shuping England**, Operations Manager
at Cyracom International, USA

UNLEASH YOUR CAREER POTENTIAL

7 Steps to Living Your Dream

KARLA BLANCO

NEW YORK

LONDON • NASHVILLE • MELBOURNE • VANCOUVER

TABLE OF CONTENTS

UNLEASH YOUR CAREER POTENTIAL
7 Steps to Living Your Dream

Published in New York, New York, by Morgan James Publishing in partnership with Difference Press. Morgan James is a trademark of Morgan James, LLC. www.MorganJamesPublishing.com

ISBN 978-1-64279-364-2 paperback
ISBN 978-1-64279-365-9 eBook
Library of Congress Control Number: 2018913763

Cover Design by:
Rachel Lopez
www.r2cdesign.com

Interior Design by:
Bonnie Bushman
The Whole Caboodle Graphic Design

In an effort to support local communities, raise awareness and funds, Morgan James Publishing donates a percentage of all book sales for the life of each book to Habitat for Humanity Peninsula and Greater Williamsburg.

Get involved today! Visit
www.MorganJamesBuilds.com

To all the brave women that take full ownership of their careers and thrive by unleashing their full potential. Easy? Of course not, but those that assume the challenge enjoy a career of significance, and it's so worth it. The world needs all those leaders to show up, bringing their full selves to the table. Looking forward to hearing about all your stories.

"Did I do enough with what was given to me?"
– Roz Hudnell

Introduction

As an author, my purpose is to open a door to those that would like to enjoy meaningful careers. For those that don't want just a job, but a place where they can add value, grow, and thrive. For those that want to find work that matters and want to leave the world in better shape than it was in when they were born.

Life surprises us in many ways and gives us many challenges. Depending on where we are in life, we are affected by our mindset (growth, stagnation, or scarcity), how we process those challenges, and how flexible we are to channel them—whether we see them as the force to continue our expansion or as a hold back, a slowdown, or something that makes us get stuck on our career journey. But the reality is that it's on us to determine how fast we move out of a challenging situation and in what direction we move.

For example, you are involved in a long transition, with many changes in it, you need to keep a strong connection with your essence and your vision, to adapt in a flexible way with a growth mindset and keep moving forward. I've been in transitions where, within two years, many groups changed in scope, managers, and team members—which also changes the group culture, priorities, and roles—but at the end of the day, how we face those situations is our choice. It's our choice to keep up and continue moving forward. Moving forward may mean re-assessing our career objectives in light of the changes or even moving to a different group or company that is in alignment with what we want to achieve in life. In order to build the career of our dreams we need to be clear on what we want, and this book will take you on a journey to clarify your purpose and priorities and define your path and dream career.

The Myth of the Promise of Education: The New Job Landscape

When we are in school, we are promised that if we choose certain specific careers we will get the income that we expect and will become happy. But nobody can tell us what our passions, values, or strengths are, which are big components of that happiness. That is something that we need to discover on a journey inside ourselves, and unless we connect the job of our dreams with our inside, that promise of happiness will hardly be conceived. Happiness doesn't come from a specific job or other external factors. All external factors can give us a temporary feeling of happiness, but as soon as we get them, that happiness fades away or only lasts as long as our "need" is perceived as satisfied.

Meanwhile, when we are able to connect with our essence and keep growing from there, the external become less important and we have more appreciation for the "small" things, like a beautiful sunset or a flower blossom.

By 2030, as many as 800 million jobs could be lost worldwide to automation, according the McKinsey report. But there will be many new jobs required—we already know that many of the careers that will exist in the future don't even exist today, just as there are many jobs today that didn't exist ten years ago, such as social media management, many online jobs, UBER drivers, and many others. The way we live, work, and get entertained is definitely changing, but then, how can you decide what will be the career of your dreams—does it exist?

To answer that question, I designed a process that will take you on a journey inside and will help you to focus on core skills, so you can overcome your current challenges but will also be able to navigate the changes that are the constant of today and the future.

Over the past two years, I've been working on "future skills," meeting with many workforce development organizations. What connects them all and makes them successful is that they have a combination of the required specific skills for a specific job with the top ten core skills. Those core skills are defined by World Economic Forum in their report of jobs of the future:

1. Complex problem solving
2. Critical thinking
3. Creativity
4. People management

5. Coordinating with others
6. Emotional intelligence
7. Judgment and decision making
8. Service orientation
9. Negotiation
10. Cognitive flexibility

Those that thrive are the ones that command the core skills. They become more successful than those in the same job that do not.

On other hand, the opportunities driven by the Internet have been changing the traditional way of work. We also have a new gig economy where anyone can have more than one job at a time. It wouldn't surprise me if this soon becomes an option in companies, too—people having more than one part time job in the same company. We are definitely in a different job landscape and I can't stress enough how important our core skills are. So, we can't sit and wait to see if any university degree will provide us with the dream job we imagined we would have. We need to get ready to get surprised by life, as sometimes life gives you opportunities that are way beyond what you imagined was the job of your dreams.

Society's Expectations

I was raised in a Latino family, and growing up this was one of the pictures of success defined by society for women: professional, married (preferably before 30 years old), at least two kids, a house, a maid (in some countries of Latin America, more than one maid!), travel for family vacations, and continuing to move up in the leadership ladder, "growing" on material possessions. Of course, this picture has some variations, and in many cases success was just defined as, get a university title, get a house, a car, a husband, and a kid. But suddenly it turns out that there are many other women, the ones that don't want to have kids, the ones that don't want a marriage, the ones that want to have more than one career and focus on that, the ones that prefer to rent a house instead of buying one because it provides more flexibility to do what they want … and let me tell you, these are trends that I am witnessing more frequently. So, is it right to think that one definition fits all? I don't think so. We all are unique and have our own priorities and it is ALL good!

Society shouldn't be telling us what can make us happy. But to stand on what we want, we first need to learn what we really want—and before that, WHO we are. That's why the process in this book starts with that, with you exploring yourself and learning what you really want, instead of just being what others told you is good for you.

> *"Be yourself, everyone else is already taken."*
> – **Oscar Wilde**

Eliminating Your Masks

When we are little kids, we quickly learn what makes our parents, our neighbors, and our friends happy. We learn that by exhibiting specific behaviors we will get rewarded or rejected, or even worse, ignored. In that quest for approval we start building different masks and roles and start, in many cases, living to please others and disconnecting from our essence. This becomes our way of identifying accepted behaviors and following role models. There's nothing wrong with learning from role models as long as your unique self is respected and is the one that shows up every day, in every message and every decision. Is that the case? What I find consistently in mentoring sessions is that people, especially women, tend to focus a lot on serving others in ways that sometimes sacrifice their own aspirations and dreams. That's why it's so important to become your own best friend. One of the techniques you'll learn in this book is the technique of the observer, and you will start asking yourself frequently: What would be my advice to me, if I were my best friend? Would I do the same? Many times, we are much more compassionate with those that surround us than we are with ourselves.

When you become the observer of your life you can identify the masks that we created in order to fit in in the office, in the society, in the world.

Warning: once you identify and start eliminating those masks, many people may leave your life, but I can assure you that the right ones will arrive, because those that resonate with your essence and your true self will be the ones that will stay. I promise, it feels like getting back home, when the people that arc aligned with your true essence start to arrive.

The master arrives when the student is ready, and that is life, a journey of learning. Every person in our life is a master and we also play that role in their lives. When the learnings are absorbed we may move forward and new people will join our journey.

The best gift that you can bring to the world is the best version of you. To be able to do that, you need to identify what masks you have acquired that may no longer serve the purpose that you are pursuing.

> *"Care about what other people think*
> *and you will always be their prisoner."*
> **– Lao Tzu**

But are all my career challenges based on society's expectations or on my own masks?

Of course not. A professional career brings a lot of different spices to our life, sometimes reflected by a project failure, a redeployment, a group closure, a leadership change of priorities, a change of incentives or job scope, a difficult boss, a company closure, etc. There are also personal challenges that can impact our career paths, and we need to be conscious of that—things like a sick person in the family, a newborn's arrival, a marriage, a divorce, a change of house, a new transit time to work, a new career, a master's degree, etc. There is an endless list of possible situations, and we all have a unique perspective on them based on our traditions, customs, and paradigms that we acquired when we were growing up from our own household or community.

All those elements define how we react to different circumstances and the level of importance that we give to them. Also, if those situations are repeatedly happening from time to time, of course we will have a different approach and at a certain point we become masters of facing them. In my case, the first time that I was involved on a redeployment process it was a very sad situation, but after being through many of them, I learned that actually, they provide an opportunity to revamp our careers, to have a fresh start and create a new life chapter.

When a group that I was leading was redeployed, I executed as expected but of course was worried about the team, knowing that they had family responsibilities. I can say that that was my dream team, a high performing team that delivered great results, which added emotion to the situation for me. Life proved to me that those high performing professionals were quickly in different jobs, learning new things and thriving as the great professionals that they are. Life is not always easy, and I know that for some people it is more difficult, but I will share with you some tools and techniques to go through situations from just wanting to revamp your career to harder situations like redeployments.

Are you ready to start the journey with me? Let's do this!

"Success is not final, failure is not fatal.
It is the courage to continue that counts."
– Winston Churchill

Chapter 1
I'VE BEEN THERE

*"I've learned that making a 'living'
is not the same thing as 'making a life.'"*
— **Maya Angelou**

Having a meaningful career can be challenging, but only you can create that career by going through a journey of self-discovery and consciousness.

What is a meaningful career? In my words, it is a career that provides me the opportunity to grow, thrive, add value, and ensure I do work that matters—that I leave the world in a better shape. It means that from my perspective, it is essential to learn about what matters to me, to be conscious that every action that I take has an impact, not only on my journey but also in the people that surround me.

Many times in the mentoring process, I got the question from a mentee: how do I connect my job, which is so mechanical, to life meaning? Let me tell you, that question usually leads to a wonderful conversation where, through meaningful questions, she identifies the why and the big impact that she is having on humanity.

Some of those questions would be: What is the company vision? If your job didn't exist, would the company reach the vision? How your job enables other groups to reach their objectives and every group as a whole acting together reaches the company vision? Every single person in the organization has a role that helps the company reach that vision. What I find many times is that people are so focused on the day-to-day that they don't connect the dots and connecting those dots is essential not only to find meaning, but also to build your elevator pitch.

Of course, there are jobs that wouldn't fit with my set of values and what I expect in life. Let me give you an example: the smoking industry. I know that I wouldn't be able to work in an industry whose products are scientifically proven to damage people's lives. That is my choice. It is my choice, because I want a world that nourishes and enriches the life of every human being on earth. I make my choices based on that perspective and I am still working on those choices.

At this point I haven't been required to work with anyone that had needed to justify or connect their purpose in life or meaningful career with an industry like that. Although my approach in life is not to judge, there are three universal principles that I apply in my life and that are part of my life compass.

Those principles are:

1. Respect everyone's opinion. This doesn't mean that I will agree with everything you tell me, but I acknowledge that the different opinions will allow us to reach a better and more inclusive solution.

2. Everyone is on their own journey. We are all at different stages in life and are here in this beautiful journey called life. A career is just a piece of that journey. Showing compassion for myself and others will allow me to understand the different moments that everyone is facing in this shared journey.

3. Compassion. Be compassionate with yourself first to understand that when you have specific non-positive feelings about a situation or a person, it is probably because there is something inside you that is ringing a bell for you to go to explore and work on that specific situation. Being compassionate is being sympathetic of others' distress, with a desire to alleviate it. We need to understand that all of us have a history behind us that has impacted the way we behave and that our perspective in life is not unique or perfect, it is a reflection of our background. With that in mind, I see others through a lens that seeks to understand behavior or situations that may be creating tension. That puts me in a neutral position instead of a position of judging.

4. Forgive. It's a simple and short word, many times so hard to process, but so important in our development and growth. Forgive yourself and forgive others. I keep recalling to myself Jesus' words: "Father, forgive them, because they do not know what they are doing" (Luke 23:34).

Let me explain to you why. I learned over the years that people don't wake up stating: "I will be mean today," or "I will do x, y, or z to this person." What I learned is that all come from a state of fear, from a state of lack of self-love, so the best that we can do is to be compassionate and forgive from the heart. This doesn't mean that you will allow a lack of respect or damage to yourself, because you need to care about you, but do what is required and forgive to move forward.

I will share my story to illustrate some of the challenges and opportunities that have helped me build a meaningful career, but it's not just my story, I asked seven amazing women to share their stories with us. You will get here a little summary of their stories, which is expanded in the coming chapters.

My Story:

In my 20-year career, I lived through and witnessed many challenges. As I advanced in the leadership ladder, of course, those challenges became bigger in terms of responsibility, impact, and complexity. A very important moment was when I decided to get certified as Vital Voices Mentor of the chapter in Costa Rica.

As a representative of the company that I work for, I attended several board of directors meetings. In one of those meetings, the board vice-president, my dear friend and mentor Alexandra Kissling, invited me and the other female board members to be part of a mentorship process for women that were owners of small businesses. She is the president of the Vital Voices Chapter in Costa Rica. Many of us joined the journey. We were recruited as accomplished business women, but what we didn't know was the impact that this process would have on our lives.

Vital Voices is a global non-governmental organization that identifies, trains, and empowers emerging women leaders and social entrepreneurs around the globe. Vital Voices looks to invest in and bring visibility to extraordinary women around the world by unleashing their leadership potential to transform lives and accelerate peace and prosperity. I've been a mentor for entrepreneurs and women at work. Mentoring is an amazing way of give yourself to others but at the same time to intensely grow by getting to know yourself better in the process.

The process took us on a journey inside ourselves, as in order to guide others we needed to know ourselves very well. This is a process, like peeling an onion, takes you layer by layer deep inside. In that process, you see things that you don't like about yourself, but also get to understand where they come from and feel empowered to change them. One revealing aspect was not feeling adequate or enough to bring my thoughts and perspectives to the business table. I discovered my cover as smart/quiet, "strategically" communicating what others wanted to hear, but as soon as I became conscious of this and identified it as a practice from childhood that I had learned to be accepted and get what I wanted, I decided to work this out in this mentoring training. The results: things started to flourish in an accelerated way. It was painful, but getting a safe space to discuss what I was going through allowed me not only to get it out of my system (my body) but also to find new ways to raise my voice, feel empowered, and to grow faster. That was the moment when I really understood that my unique thoughts and perspectives were not only valuable, but required. They were not always appreciated by everyone, but it's okay because I am showing up now sharing my own perspective and adding more value, which also helped me to move faster in the leadership ladder. The mentoring process is not about giving solutions but guiding the mentees with significant questions to reach their own goals.

As mentor and mentee, I learned that many times the challenge that arose in the moment was just the tipping point of something bigger and deeper, but the key element on all this is the inside. As we discover our essence, we also learn that all the answers are inside us.

Another key moment was when I was called to become Aspen Institute fellow under the Central American Leadership Initiative (CALI). Every year a diverse cohort of proximately 23 people is selected to start a journey that takes them from leadership to significance. That was especially important as in my job, I was part of the team that was leading a layoff for the company and although there were very clear business objectives on my plate and I am a focused person delivering results, there were also many people that would be impacted by the process, which of course meant pain to me. Of course, those processes are managed with a lot of confidentiality and you are very lonely in the process that can sometimes take many months. This fellowship came just in time to become a relief in the middle of a hard process, during which time I appreciated the full support that I got from my manager. This was a relief because, as part of the fellowship, we deeply explored our leadership styles, our moral compasses, and our footprints on the world and actually made a social impact commitment with a diverse cohort, understanding that all of us face the same leadership and human challenges. The members of that cohort became brothers and sisters of my heart, and I certainly became more a Central American and global citizen after this transformational process.

I highlight those two moments as transformative moments in the journey back home to my essence and in learning more about myself to become a better leader and human being.

My family support has been essential in my career. There are not enough words of appreciation for the support received from my parents, my siblings, my aunt Ofe, and other aunts, uncles, and cousins, like Jhise.

Although we are told many times that we need to separate the personal stuff from work, the reality is that we are holistic multidimensional human beings. We are a package, so understanding the different "pockets" of our life and having awareness helps us to better manage different situations.

Through the book I share many stories from myself and my mentees, as those are rich examples and, just by accompanying them in their own journeys, I learned that many teams have the same general challenges or questions—though I also learned that all situations are unique as we all are unique and have different needs.

I moved from Costa Rica to United States back in 2017 and new mentees keep coming to me, so I decided to create the seven-step workshop that I summarize in this book and guide them on a process to identify their current challenges and build the career of their dreams.

Others that Have Been through the Inner Journey Process:

- Shirlene. Young, determined professional. She was finishing her career and applied to a position that was perfect for her profile. She was nervous but with strong presence and high composure made it through the interview and started the career of her dreams. She later got married and had two beautiful kids, Saul and Sofia. They became her drive and strength. Always easy? No. She required support in order to keep growing and keep her family growth, too. Gerardo, her husband, has been essential in the process. Both have balanced family tasks and responsibilities in order to face life demands.

  Shirlene is a structured, perfectionist person that strives to always deliver her best. She started as an individual contributor but today has more than ten people reporting to her and keeps wiggling and finding ways to ensure the best quality and amazing growth for herself and her team.

- Natalia. A young engineer who started as a student worker and has faced several transitions since year one. Her ability to adapt, be flexible, and pursue her passion has taken her through paths that even she didn't imagine. This may sound like an easy path, but trust me, she opened her mind and heart to flow with life, overcoming many challenges. She defined what she wanted, asked for it, and got on the path of the career of her dreams, inspiring many other girls to follow their own dreams. Naty, as we call her, is single, lives with her family, and is very close to her brother.

- Angie. A natural leader. The kind of heart that is always looking for ways to help others. Passionate about professional women's progression and diversity, becoming a national leader of reference in that topic. She has been intentional in her career, moving up the ladder but taking the time to follow her passion, opening doors and creating opportunities for women to advance and engage in technical careers. She has gone through professional challenges, as we all have, but I would call her the unstoppable—she finds ways to keep moving. I want to highlight that Angie knows how to ask for help and reach out to whoever can provide that help. Angie is married and has one daughter.

- Fernanda. A dynamo. Always delivering the best and investing in her growth, which has payoff as she continuously reaches her dreams. Give her a small project and she will create an unimaginable impact with results beyond the expected. Life challenged Fernanda when her group was closed, but within a month she got a new job and now is looking for her next big opportunity. She is married and has two sons that are attending university. Fernanda's approach to life is to work hard but enjoy as much as she can. She always has a smile and can-do attitude.

- Masayo. Structured, disciplined. Integrity is her personal brand. She has been through many tough challenges in life, but her husband and sons are always a great motive to keep moving ahead. The same year that she lost her father, she burned her feet and went through a painful treatment in recovery. On top of that, she lost her job, a job where she was bright as a star, a job that fulfilled her due to the social impact that she was driving. While she was sad at the moment she received the news, she took her time to think and decide what she wanted, didn't rush herself, and landed in a job where all her talents and strengths are recognized. Now she is back building strategies to create a social impact.

- Andrea. She moved to the US a few years ago looking for growth opportunities and has been growing but not alone. Andrea's leadership brought many along with her, opening doors and opportunities for others. I am one of those, as she opened many doors for me when I landed in the US in 2017. She is an impressive leader. When I arrived, I didn't know many people and, although she has fewer years of professional experience than I do, she has a strong network where we live and took me into her networks, giving me the opportunity to connect with new people. Not only that, but she is an amazing women's advocate. She is married. Her husband agreed to support her career growth by taking care of the kids until they grow up and he can return to work. They have two kids and a baby coming.

• Erika. Happy and committed by nature. She's that kind of person who, as soon as you meet her, you connect. Her first offer is a big smile, that smile that has helped her face big challenges in life. She has been engaged with the government, private sector, and academia. She loves to meet new people and help people. Her personal brand is to deliver results and learn whatever is necessary to get things done. She met her husband in high school, but they got engaged later, after they finished university. She has a daughter who is her life motor and inspiration.

While I was writing about these amazing women, I was telling myself about how fortunate I've been to have women like them in my life. Women who not only have a positive outlook on life, but also have the determination to keep growing, despite the circumstances and challenges that life brings—and guess what? They not only overcome their challenges, but they keep expanding their footprint by taking the others around them, ensuring others grow with them. I will share with you more about their challenges in the following chapters, but I didn't want to wait to share a little bit about them since I know you may identify with them.

Chapter 2

A Toolkit to Build the Career of Your Dreams

*"And when your journey seems too hard, and when
you run into a chorus of cynics who tell you that
you're being foolish to keep believing or that you can't
do something, or that you should just give up, or you
just settle—you might say to yourself a little phrase
that I've found handy these last eight years:
Yes, we can."*
– **Barack Obama** to Harvard University in 2016

A s I've been through many situations during these twenty plus years of my professional career, I got a collection of tools that helped me to overcome the difficult times. This is a process that you will start with me in this book, but you can always come back and re-use the tools required in any specific situation. Actually, the intention is that some of them become natural to your day-to-day. You will get surprised and proud of yourself when you start seeing in yourself the change that you want to see in the world.

At this point, I would like to ask you to find a notebook and colored pens, as you will be answering questions throughout this whole process and it is always helpful to highlight what you want to recall in the future. If you prefer, you can use a computer or any other device to record your process, but it has been demonstrated that writing on paper creates a special neurological connection in our brains and, even if you don't go back to your notes, they become like a stamp in the brain. But remember, this is your process and it's your choice. I will just keep highlighting throughout the process what works best for me and my mentees.

The toolkit starts with a reflection where you will identify what you think your current challenges are, which usually brings up additional ones or simply leads us to learn that what we thought was a challenge is really not.

The Process

This is a process that will guide you to learn deeply about yourself, to learn about the choices that you are making and what possible implications they will have in your future. You will learn about which expectations you have been meeting so far and you will define what your new expectations are. You will invite the elephant in the room to become visible, revealing your fears, your aspirations. You will peel yourself like an onion, getting to the core of who you really are, after taking all the masks off and defining what you really want. But this is not a passive process. I want you to commit to yourself, to love yourself and to bring your full self to the table.

We will see life happening and challenges coming to our way but there will be always the opportunity to come back to the process and apply some of the techniques to get back on track.

This is a summary of the seven-step process that we will be using in this book to unleash your career potential:

1. Step One: The mirror and the observer. First, you will recognize the stranger in the mirror. Sometimes we get so busy and allow complexity to join us in a way that when we see ourselves in the mirror we don't even recognize ourselves or we avoid seeing ourselves in the mirror. When we reach the point of looking in the mirror every day and feeling comfortable with ourselves, we will step into the back seat and become an active observer. Being the observer allows us to make new neurological connections to manifest the career that we want. Being conscious of every thought and action allows us to become aware and intentional. Becoming the observer of our life and knowing that we got our power back will allow us to design the career of our dreams, and to perform to the role of CEO (Chief Executive Officer) of our lives.

2. Step Two: Learn about your career cycles and design your career. We all have career cycles, whether we have them clear or not. If you are at the beginning of your career we can still analyze some of the life situations that move us in different directions and will probably lead you into your cycles. In this step of the process we identify who is part of our journey. Are we missing anyone in our master plan? We will test the coherence between our own values and the values of the company that we work for. I'll show you the 1/5/10 exercise, which will allow you to plan on one page your career for the next ten years. To end this step, you will define your career manifesto. What do you envision at the end of life your career footprint?

3. Step Three: Board of Advisors. There are many people in your career that will help you to advance. There may be others that can also delay you, but during this step you will learn how to identify those current members of your Board of Advisors, move away from some, and invite others, according to the career that you designed.

4. Step Four: The power of serving. In this chapter we will decode the big return on investment of service in our careers. We will demystify: "This is not my scope" or "I don't have time." By serving others we impact our way in some or many ways. Of course, a balance is required as you must first know what you want and why you want it. So, you do it intentionally. When you are aware of what you want and you volunteer yourself

to relieve someone by serving and contributing to their objectives, you are not only serving others you are also serving yourself and your career path.

5. Step Five: Your voice. The ripple effect of your personal brand. Whether you are aware or not, you have a personal brand. People perceive it since that first impression. Sometimes we think one thing of ourselves that doesn't necessarily matches others' perceptions. We will assess your current brand and check if it's in alignment with what you want and with your future self and, at the same time, we will identify your voice as a propulsion and force of your brand.

6. Step Six: The world needs you. Release the best version of you. We will work in this chapter to go a step deeper into your values, strengths, emotions, and passions. Your full self is the best gift that you can give to the world and this is a continuous exercise of awareness and conquering yourself to ensure that the best version of you shows up to the world every day.

7. Step Seven: Life happens. Resilience is how you reconnect to your journey. Life is not a steady and linear journey. It has its peaks and valleys and I will share with you some techniques for when those difficult moments come to the game. We will work on strengthening your resiliency so it becomes a natural muscle that is ready to be activated as soon as life hits us and we need to get back to our path. We need to ensure we keep moving forward.

8. Practical hacks. At the end of the process I will share some of my personal practices that keep me up and engaged in showing up as the CEO of my career.

To get into the process we go on a voyage of self-discovery, learning what serves us and what ideas from childhood or from any parts of our lives don't serve us any longer. We need a laser-focused view on those, but it's a matter of questioning ourselves to let them come to the surface and then deciding if in our new design of our future self those are still adding value or if we need to let them go.

You will get many tools and techniques and, since life is an evolving path, you can always come back and use the process for many other challenges in life for you or for others.

Chapter 3

THE MIRROR AND
THE OBSERVER

"Be the change that you want to see in the world."
– Gandhi

What is the mirror?

We can't change what we don't know and our pace in life has been significantly accelerated, which sometimes makes it challenging for us to take a simple pause, even a pause just to see ourselves in the mirror. We get many demands in our day-to-day and we become too busy delivering results and keeping up with many expectations. Some days, life is just wake up, quick coffee, jump into the bus, train, or car to the office, lunch at our desk (sometimes in the car depending on our schedule)—and we don't even stop to see ourselves in the mirror. The days keep moving forward and we enter into a vicious circle until we hit reality and decide to take ownership and assign the right priorities. I don't mean that work is not a priority, but work over you is not the right priority. I see work as a means to keep developing myself, to keep learning new things and to connect with my life purpose, but I find out that there are too many people surviving instead of living to their fullest. It is not that I've been always in this place—there have been periods in my life that I've been in that mechanical cycle—and I am grateful for the moment that I decided to take my first step towards uncertainty, taking the risk of even possibly losing my job, but knowing that I couldn't spend more time just filling the blank spaces of my day.

I started my career in a Fortune 100 company as a customs and free trade zone analyst. My English was very basic, but I think that my first boss saw beyond the obvious. I remember even making signs with my hands for those words in English that weren't coming to me in the interview, and I am sure that my passion came through. On my first day, I asked my boss about his expectations and where I could find what I needed to deliver. His answer was, "I hired you because you know what needs to be done." At that moment I felt weird, but actually it was a passport of freedom and empowerment.

I moved forward, until there was a need in accounting. Since I am a learner, I thought that it would be an amazing experience, but I quickly learned that I didn't like crunching numbers. I had had a conversation with the manager at that time and he was very open. They allowed me to keep my focus in customs. I felt very happy, as customs was my expertise and I didn't enjoy the accounting experience. This was a great experience as a process to learn what I want and what I don't want.

A couple of years later an opportunity knocked on my door, supporting the public affairs manager in setting up some learning sessions for employees. Given my external network and background, it was a perfect fit. The company wanted its employees to make an informed decision, so I was in charge of bringing experts to share different perspectives and clarify doubts for them. This was not an official job, but it was a way to channel my passion. I enjoyed the experience and continued supporting the public affairs manager until the controller told me that I needed to make a decision to move to the other department or tell him if I committed to come back full time to my previous position within the next three months. He stated: you don't need to worry about losing a job as in the factory there may be many options including cleaning floors" (of course he was being sarcastic). At that point I was fired up with the work that was being done in the Public Affairs Department. From my conversation with the department manager I learned that there was a possibility to open the government affairs position. She required the corporate approval, but I assumed the risk and told the controller that he could open the customs position to fulfill my replacement as I was not planning to go back to finance.

Doing something that I didn't like (the accounting) and then doing something that I felt so passionate about gave me the strength to take the risk and bet for my passion. It turned out that the government affairs position was open, I applied, I got interviewed, and at the end got the position. Looking back in retrospect, this was a time when I was faced with a mirror, looking to my eyes and my passion. The mirror is not something tangible, it is a reflection on our life and at that time it came up very clearly which was my passion.

The mirror can be a real one or a figurative one. Have a five-minute daily conversation (you can set your phone time keeper) with yourself, fresh in the morning, and ask: What do I want? What am I willing to do to follow my dreams? Are those really my dreams or someone's else?

Do this exercise for a week and take notes on what is coming to you in this process. Don't judge, just take notes, and on day seven you will review them again and check if anything has changed. Keep doing this for at least 21 days, so this becomes a habit.

You can also ask a person that you love and trust to engage with you in a fifteen-minute conversation about your dreams and what you want. If this is your choice, I just want you to set three basic expectations for the process:

1. This is a private conversation among the two of you,
2. No judgment is accepted, as this is a creative process for you, and
3. They can't reflect their dreams or fears on you and if they do (as we all are humans), you need to show appreciation but move forward and look deep into yourself, to understand what you really want.

In Chapter 10, I give you a practical hack (daily practice) that has really helped me to clarify my thoughts about what I really want.

What is the observer?

If you really embraced the mirror concept and already started to explore it, wait until you see the power of the observer.

I call the process where you become a third party in your own life "the observer." You start becoming more present and aware of your actions because you observe and start to listen, not only with your ears but with all your senses. That process leads us to live a more conscious life and to become more responsible for taking action versus reacting to things.

In the past, I used to have a daily review of my day before I went to bed. Nowadays, I still do that, but add in my observation of the moment, and it has enriched my perspective and my way of living in many ways.

There are some rules for the observer:

1. Invite compassion to the table. Understand that we all are in a journey and have a past which has shaped us, from the stereotypes and patterns from our families and communities. Just focus on observing and taking notes.

2. Don't judge. As a compassionate person that understands that we all have a background that influences us, respect every action and don't engage in judging the situation or actions from others.

3. Don't jump to conclusions. Just observe.

As the observer, take notes of the day's main events and indicate the emotions that you experienced. At the end of the day, you will use the notes to analyze your own reactions and those observations will become a mirror and help you to adjust your behaviors and actions, aligning them to your journey purpose. If at this point you are not clear about your purpose, don't worry—it will be more clear in the coming chapters—but still take notes, because it will help you define that purpose.

The observer takes a look at everything, including how your time is being invested. (You will do that in chart 1). When I say, "take a look of everything," this includes thoughts and words. That gives you an important hint about your current mindset: is it a scarcity and negative mindset, or is it a growth mindset that leads you to seize opportunities? Remember, all the notes and observations have the objective to serve your purpose. You are not required to share them. Those notes are gifts of awareness that you are giving to yourself.

The Power of Observation

As a result of an observation, Angie transformed one of her biggest career challenges into her next big career step. Her main observation: strengthen her listening skills.

Angie's passion is helping people and problem solving. That's why she's engaged in diversity and inclusion as co-chair of the Women Network in Costa Rica. She is a warrior that embraces all kinds of justice causes.

She started her professional journey as a customer care supervisor in a call center. She later moved to a Fortune 100 company where she started as an agent of the call center, but after her first year became a systems analyst. Her leadership skills opened doors for her to become a manager, and for the last two years she has been chief of staff and operations manager.

Although she works in the Information Technology group, her academic background is in social science, which provides her with a different perspective. All of her career has been deployed in that group and her data analysis strength, deep observation, context understanding, and problem solving have enabled her growth path. She acquired her technical knowledge while working, driving her own research, reading, asking, and looking for mentors.

She faced several challenges due to her direct approach, to the point that she was at risk of losing her job, but her former boss was able to look beyond that and trusted her. Due to that situation, she learned and adopted a different approach, strengthening her listening and observer skills and getting the help of people that provided her with hope and guidance to learn and keep moving forward without leaving the company.

Angie's determination and faith keep her moving forward, helping others reach their dreams and making a difference for those in need. She practices the observer and using the mirror with her Board of Advisors and those that surround her.

Which expectations am I meeting?

As part of our observation process we will implement the following exercise: for seven days, fill in the "My day-to-day" chart. At the end of day seven, tell yourself what you've found.

As you become the observer of your life, you start realizing which expectations you are meeting. That is very easy to identify, but it requires the help of the mirror and the observer. As you reach the seventh day of the mirror exercise, you will open your notes and you will assess how many hours of your days you are investing in the following categories:

CHART 1: My Day-to-Day

CHART 1
MY DAY TO DAY

	ACTION	Day 1	Day 2	Day 3	Day 4	Day 5	Day 6	Day 7
1	Sleep							
2	Physical exercise							
3	Eat (YES! It's important)							
4	Spiritual practice (pray, meditate, church, etc.)							
5	Significant other—shared time							
6	Family time							
7	If you have kids—how much time did you spend with them?							
8	Friend time							
9	Hobby time							
10	Work							
11	Traffic time (any transportation required during the day)							
12	Other activities (list them): _____							

All of those categories have a place in our lives and meet expectations. For example, not everyone needs eight hours of sleep, but to keep a healthy life, you shouldn't get less than six hours, unless you have a special condition that you are aware of before doing this exercise. All of the categories show important categories in life, but the time (which is life investment) assigned to each category will tell you which expectations you are meeting and will provide you with perspective on how you are currently investing your time and how you would really like to invest your time. Later we will come back to this section as we need to check our schedule day-to-day.

List of choices. Am I surviving or thriving?

Now that you have clear how you, in general, invest your time, I would like you to have a self-reflection on the question:

Am I surviving or thriving? I call it surviving when more than 70% of our day is spent on work, so you are in the vicious cycle of wake up, go to work, get back home, go back to sleep, and repeat every day during the workweek. Saturdays are used to run all the errands that were not possible during the week. If that sounds like you, I would like you to take notes to answer the following questions:

1. Are you happy with your current time assignment? Would you adjust anything to show your priorities in the time assignment?
2. If money were not an issue, what would your days look like?
3. Would you make some adjustments in order to ensure that you have a better quality of life? Or are you happy with what is currently reflected in your day-to-day?
4. Are you willing to prioritize your health? What would be the first step in that direction? Or maybe the chart already shows that. What is your case?

5. Are you proud of your current time distribution?
6. Is your current time distribution purposely defined to reach your life purpose?
7. According to your time distribution, whose expectations are you meeting?
8. Are you surviving or thriving in life? Do you live a life of joy?

Fill out the chart, assigning the ideal time allocation to meet your life expectations:

CHART 2
PRIORITIES

	ACTION	IDEAL DAY HOURS ALLOCATED BY ACTIVITY	ASSIGN A NUMBER OF PRIORITY FROM 1 (TOP PRIORITY) TO 12 (LOWEST PRIORITY)
1	Sleep		
2	Physical exercise		
3	Eat (YES! It's important)		
4	Spiritual practice (pray, meditate, church, etc.)		
5	Significant other—shared time		
6	Family time		
7	If you have kids—how much time did you spend with them?		
8	Friend time		
9	Hobby time		
10	Work		
11	Traffic time (any transportation required during the day)		
12	Other activities (list them): _____		

The Role of Significance in Our Life

A life of significance is a life that has a footprint in the world, a life that makes a difference. But that is not possible if you don't know yourself deeply and live your life with intention and purpose.

Significance means that you know what your purpose is in life and align your activities to what you want in life. It means that you have coherence between what you expect and what you do every day to meet your expectations. It means that you value yourself and your time. That you assign the right priorities for you. There is no general right or wrong. You are the one that defines what is significant for you, what is important and meaningful according to your unique journey and circumstances. It means that you already know what that purpose is. If this is not clear yet, don't worry, because by the end of this book you will have it clear. If you are happy in the cycle of wake up, work, sleep, wake up, work, and sleep again, over and over, it is up to you and nobody can judge you, but if you are reading this book, I am pretty sure that you want MORE in your life and we are here to work that out together. By now, I just ask you to list your passions. We will touch on that later in the book.

Your Future: You Are the CEO of Your Life

As you arrive at this point you may be already wondering, or maybe just confirming, what you already have had in mind for your future. You should be the one deciding how you want your life in the future to go, or others will make that decision for you. In that case, you would be helping others to reach their dreams but not necessarily living your own dreams. There's nothing wrong with helping others to reach their dreams, as long as you are meeting yours.

You are the Chief Executive Officer of your life and so you are required to define your vision and objectives. As part of your life objectives, your career objectives play an important role in reaching that vision. If you dream of impacting lives, generating jobs for people by being an entrepreneur, and you are today a worker in a company, how do you ensure that you learn all that you need to become that entrepreneur while being conscious of the sacrifices that are required? Don't get me wrong, being a company worker also include sacrifices, and that's why it's so important to have a clear vision so that you can put it all in perspective and can thrive and live your purpose.

Please take your notebook or workbook out again. We will start working on that future definition and, as it is easier to understand a life backwards, you will work in your obituary, understanding how you want to be remembered. Remember, this is a work in progress, and the obituary you write today may require some adjustments when you finish reading this book. That's all right, but we need to take the first step and define, according to what you want for your future, how you want to be remembered. What are those key memories that you want to leave in the lives of your loved ones, in your community, in your country, in the world? Bring that purpose and significance to your life.

If you find this exercise difficult, I invite you to take out one hour in your agenda and tag it as your vision hour. In that hour, you can do several things: find a big white paper or a board to collect pictures from magazines, or Google some and print them, or cut and paste those images to create an online vision board. This is a time for you to pick and choose what those moments are that you want to live. How do you see yourself: alone or with a family, maybe some friends, kids, dogs, horses? Just enjoy the moment and, once you finish it, think and write about how you would like to be remembered. Who will read your obituary the day that you transcend? What is your footprint? All time you invest in yourself is very valuable to reach your vision as CEO of your life.

LEARN ABOUT YOUR
CAREER CYCLES AND
DESIGN YOUR CAREER

*"If you don't design your own life plan, chances
are you'll fall into someone else's plan. And guess
what they have planned for you? Not much."*
– Jim Rohn

A career is defined by the series of positions and jobs that we perform throughout our work life. Since we are the CEO of our life and by now we have a clear vision of what we want in our life, we will start the process of designing our career path.

In order to design our career path, we will define some basic elements. You are free to add any others that may be meaningful for you. When we define career elements, we will proceed to map our career cycles and will assess the alignment of our values against the company values. Once we have all that clear we will design our 1/5/10 to finally connect the dots and make our career commitment.

Career path elements:

1. Life Vision & Mission. Life is the greatest gift that we get and it's our responsibility to define what we want and how we want to live that life. The vision provides us a north, tells what we want from our life, and the mission for how we will get there. In my case:

    My vision: Live a life of meaning and significance

    My mission: Continuously grow and thrive by connecting, lifting, and being lifted by my journey fellows.

2. Your core competencies. This is a combination of skills and abilities that makes you unique. You need to clearly identify and clearly articulate your current competencies in a simple but clear way. Let's pick your top 5.

    Some examples: Leadership, Collaboration, Problem Solving, Negotiation, Networking, Data Management, Mentoring, Coaching, Cognitive Flexibility, Structured Thinking, Creative Thinking, Influencing, Strategizing, Communication, Research, Results-Oriented, Ethics, Technical skills (specific to a career or position: like coding, accounting, 3D printing, designing, etc.).

3. The landscape. Usually we are so focused on our day-to-day delivery that we miss what is going on in our external environment or even in other departments of where we work. We need the discipline to continuously map what is going on—get out of your bubble! This means that if in your career map you have as an objective a specific move, get out and meet the experts that are already doing the job, get to meet their customers and stakeholders. Map that internally to the company but also externally, look for different business chambers, and understand how this role is being performed in other places. This may give you additional perspective and advance your possibilities to get to that next position.

Read research, white papers, books, articles, blogs, and posts around the job and understand what is going on inside and outside the company.

4. Job profiles. There is a set of your core competencies and skills that are transferable through different jobs. Get to understand and define what those are, so you can look for different job opportunities. Sometimes, we get stuck in one job description and once we have clear what the core competencies are, the landscape of job profiles gets expanded into many more. When you look for job descriptions for your next move, put those key competencies in the search engine and a big list of possibilities will come out. Read the job descriptions and select those that are most appealing to you, but at

this point you will have more than three to five options to look for. Pick your top three.

5. Training and development opportunities required. As you already identified the top three jobs that you may be interested in moving forward in your career, get to understand what some development opportunities are that can bring you forward as the top candidate for the position. Look for potential formal and informal training. Get prepared for that opportunity.

6. The network. When you did the landscape analysis, you identified the job partners, customers and stakeholders. Now is the time to ensure that you intentionally connect with them. Meet them, get curious to learn how their days look, how they arrived where they are. Be honest and kind and continue to nurture that relationship. Provide follow up to your conversation as appreciation of their time with you. Volunteer yourself to help with projects that connect with the positions you're interested in, so that you have more possibilities to expand your network and for them to get to know you better and see what you can achieve for them.

7. Show who you are: Focus on your resume and your short and long bio. In our current environment, with busy agendas and many candidates applying to positions, people read resumes doing a quick scan of the first half page and maybe going to the end or quickly scanning the rest of the document to see if anything interesting pops up. An appealing resume requires a

time investment. Go to your performance evaluations and get those important achievements that you feel proud of, but ensure that you put the achievement first, including numbers (such as savings, cost avoidance, number of people impacted, time reduced, and any other indicators).

The person that is recruiting will look at those rather than at long descriptions. Your resume shouldn't be more than two pages and it must be relevant to the position. Take a look at the job descriptions that you choose and use the same language.

The other two important documents that you must have at hand are your short bio (no more than 50 words) and your long bio (no more than 250 words). This is very helpful for when you are trying to connect with people to learn about a position or even to get an interview. Send an email and use your short bio to introduce yourself. If you don't have those documents ready, in Chapter 8 we will be building those.

Career Cycles

A career cycle shows a person's trend to transition or change jobs. If you are clear about what your career cycles are, you can intentionally better prepare yourself for your next move, even when you are starting a new job. I have told my last three managers what I am looking for in for my next move, and they became very good allies on that movement. Nowadays, those cycles, are usually shorter than in the past. In my 20+ years of career I have performed seven different jobs; meanwhile, my mom in her 40+ year career performed around four different jobs and I am sure that now that we are in the gig economy those numbers will easily be multiplied twice or three times. There are even people performing more than one job at a time. The number of jobs is not as relevant as the value that understanding your cycles brings for you to get prepared in advance and not get surprised when you are heading toward an end of one and you are already looking for new options.

When I did this exercise, I thought that I didn't have important clear cycles and identified two long cycles of eight years with a couple of transitional years in between. There are other people that, for example, have the personal need to change every two years the job. In my case, as long as I keep learning, feel productive adding value, and flourish, I can stay as long as eight years (or maybe more) in the same position. The exercise was very relevant, as I discovered what my triggers were when I felt that I needed a change, and it consistently aligns with situations where I had a boss that put me in a box, a boss for whom it's their way or no other way. But in addition to that, which I think we all at some point of our career have the rich experience to have those kind of bosses, I also identified that since I am a learner and my mission is to have a continuous development path, those new learnings have led me to new positions. So, by mapping your career cycles you will learn a lot about yourself.

Those career cycles also map big significant events of your life such as engagement, marriage, newborns, family member illness, lost, new career start, Masters, PhD, city change, or any event that may have an impact on your day-to-day.

Are you ready? Let's get started.

Open your notebook, workbook, or, if you prefer to color and use all your creativity, grab a big paper with pens or colored pencils to put color to your career map.

For example,

Identifying Career Cycles

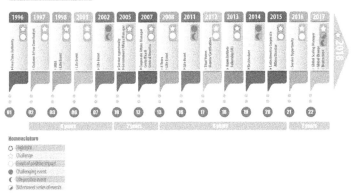

Where am I today in my cycle? Do I want to keep it or change my cycle?

To define your cycles, create your map, writing down year by year the different jobs that you have had as well as your important life moments, such as university graduations, new studies, marriage, births, losses, and any other life events that you consider relevant. We are multidimensional beings and all our dimensions are interconnected and impact one another. Once you have the map, take a look as an observer. There are people that stay longer than a decade in one job. Even if you spend a decade in a job, I'll bet that there are important events that change your job and impact your life in that time, such as adoption of a new system, addition of functions, boss change, etc. You name it.

Once you defined your cycles and are able to map relevant life situations, respond in your workbook to the following questions:

1. What do I see? Do I see a clear trend in my cycles?
2. Am I in one of those points of transition and change?
3. What do I want to see next in my next new cycle? When do I want that to happen?
4. Is there any personal event that I can anticipate coming and impacting my cycle?
5. Highlight the event in your map that makes you feel very proud. Describe the moment, why you felt so proud, and what the key skills were that helped you get there.
6. Describe which the lowest point on that map was and what lessons you learned. What are the changes that you are taking in your life to prevent that situation? There are situations that certainly are out of your control, but how you react to them can make a huge difference in how you go through and end the process.
7. Take the answer to question 3 and describe how you look at yourself. Delighted? Proud? Happy? Who will be with you in that future moment? What does the celebration of the moment look like?

Now that you have your career cycle mapped, let's understand who is part of your current journey and how they contribute to your vision. Do you want to keep them in?

The career path is not a lonely journey. It can be, but an isolated journey decreases our growth opportunities and its richness. Please take a look at your career map again and name five key people that were with you in those key transition moments. Who is still involved in your journey? Do you want to keep them with you? We need to be selective about who joins our journey, because trust me, if you surround yourself with people that have a scarcity mindset it will be harder to move forward—and on the other hand, people that uplift you and are able to see and nurture your potential will help you accelerate your next move of growth. I would like you to also name three people that you haven't met yet but that you know can connect you with your next move, connecting you with others or even becoming your next boss. Yes, you can pick who will be your next boss!

When you meet those three people, ask them to provide you with three names of other people who may be relevant in your process, and now you have twelve new people in your network, just by being intentional. Master the meaningful networking process! A way to map those specific people is to map the connections within the department or company where you want to work. Do your homework—it has a big return on investment. Take a look at the position and what the connections are, reach out to people that are connected to that position—coworkers, customers, people that have performed the position. If you don't have any connections, go to LinkedIn and make those connections. Ask for ten minutes on someone's calendar and ensure that you have your one-minute elevator pitch ready before your call. Prepare two questions and follow up on the connection with an email or LinkedIn thank you message. Remember to nurture your connections.

In the next chapter, we will talk about our Board of Advisors and how important it is that we intentionally set up a vibrant and relevant Board of Advisors to help us maneuver our careers. There are many roles that people can play in your life, from the inspiration leader to the strategist or realistic member of your Board of Advisors.

The company values and my values. Am I in the right place?

"When your values are clear to you,
making decisions become easier."
– Roy E. Disney

Coherence is the quality of being consistent. When your strengths, passions, actions, and values are aligned and are showing up consistently in your day-to-day, you are in coherence.

Coherence bring us happiness and peace. When we are in coherence, we feel safe and we can thrive.

Values are the principles or standards that guide our life. They are the core of our moral compass, and help us define what is right and what is wrong.

That's why it's so important to do our homework before we decide to join any company. We really need to understand the company's culture and its core values, because if they are in alignment with our own values we can soar. If we don't find that balance, we can end up living the nightmare of our lives.

The company where I work has a culture that embraces diversity, creating an inclusive work environment where everyone is treated equally with dignity and respect. It so happened that a manager was hired. He showed high technical expertise and very good external engagement, but he didn't value the equal treatment for everyone. He wanted a reserved parking space for him and someone that could make photocopies for him and bring him coffee to his desk. Those small details mattered for him and didn't make him feel happy. Although he got results, he didn't fit into a company that treats everyone as equal, so he left in less than a year.

In Chapter 8, we will do an exercise to understand your values and use them as a powerful tool in your career development. I wanted to highlight them here because, although you can identify three options for jobs, you need to be aware about the culture and values of a potential company, business group, or organization to evaluate if it is a good fit for you. In some cases, people don't feel fulfilled, and just by doing this assessment they get to understand that although they may like their job, the values mismatch brings a lack of coherence into their lives. It is better for them to find a place where they can get that coherence.

The 1/5/10 Process

> *"Setting goals is the first step in*
> *turning the invisible into visible."*
> **– Tony Robbins**

Setting goals gives you clarity and allows you to get focus. In the past, it was very uncomfortable for me to get into conversations with my managers about getting those specific goals for my career development. I had no issues at all in getting work goals for the year and on a quarterly basis, but when it was about career development, I had problems. I came from two parents who made long careers in very specific positions, and I didn't get why I was required to develop new career goals, as I was happy in my position. Then I decided to make a different move, and what worked for me was to set up my 1/5/10 process, which defines what I am willing and what I am not willing to do in my next one year, five years and ten years. For some people, it is important to paint even where they see themselves in twenty years, so, from there, they go backwards, defining what they see themselves doing 20 years from now, 15, and ten years from now. My preference is ten years, and that's why I focus on the 1/5/10.

This is a high-level process that provides me with guidance for my next decade of my career and specific smart goals for the coming year. That made a huge difference, and nowadays I use this as my map of the future. What is interesting to me is that once I got relieved of being so specific and I defined what I was willing to do and what I was not willing to do in the next year, in the next five years, and in the next ten years, that is when I got a pull in of the results. I completed all of my smart goals defined for year one and finished many of the five-year goals during year one—and many of the next ten years' goals during year five.

What happens here is that you start organizing your thoughts and actions purposely and acting intentionally, because you have a map, a guide, and it's not left in the hands of fortune. You seize your opportunities, because you know what you want and what you are willing to do.

When you ask yourself, "What do I want next?" I hope you feel fired up to go and do whatever is necessary to get that next job, and in order to do that you had better have not only value coherence but also a strong passion, because you know that your next job will get you closer to your life vision.

Are you with me? Bring your workbook, open your computer, or grab a paper to start the process. Once you get it done, take a picture and keep that 1/5/10 close to you as a reminder of where you are moving toward.

I will use my 2012 example so that you can get a clear picture of what I want you to put on your chart.

Think about what you want and also what you are willing or not willing to do in order to get there. Maybe there's something that you can't commit to in year one because of life circumstances, but you can commit to it in year five or year ten. This is a brainstorming exercise with yourself, but if there are things that may affect others in your family, talk to them and share your thoughts; for example, if you are willing to move abroad in three to five years, tell them and ask them. There are no better supporters than family, but they must be considered if they may become impacted by your plans, for example, if you are thinking to move to a different city or country. It may sound obvious, but I found cases where this was not considered and created unnecessary tension in the family.

CHART 3: 1/5/10
Karla 2012

CHART 3
1/5/10
Karla 2012

YEAR 1	YEAR 5	YEAR 10
1. Support the Regional Latin American Director on people's development plans	1. Become the Regional Director	1. Transition to a Corporate Global position
2. Rotation to a corporate position	2. Build a high performing team	2. Develop a high performing team
3. Strengthen my regional network	3. Extend my global network	3. Strengthen my global network
4. Live in Costa Rica	4. Live in Costa Rica	4. Open to leave Costa Rica

For many people, this maybe a too high-level or general a chart, but for me it worked out perfectly, as I wasn't very clear on what specific job or position I would want back in 2012, but I was clear that I wanted to keep myself learning and growing. This process of defining high level priorities helped me shape what came afterwards.

Year 1: 2012. I was running the workgroup for Costa Rica and Central America. One of my life passions has been to support people's development by helping them to unleash their potential, which is why I offered myself to help my regional boss to do that exercise I mentioned earlier with the whole regional team. That helped me understand what their aspirations and struggles were. We set up plans for every team member, and this process helped me to strengthen my regional network.

During that year, I didn't get any rotation opportunity, as I was required to focus on my Costa Rican/ Central American job due to a big restructuring that started to be planned during 2013 (Year 2) and required full execution in 2014 (Year 3). The rotation opportunity came in 2014, and I spent three months covering a corporate position.

In 2015 (Year 4), I got the regional position and developed a high-performing team for the region, aligning them to corporate priorities and delivering amazing results for the region. In 2016, I had the opportunity to get engaged on the development of a new signature program. A team member covered my position while I focused on the project. In March 2017, I applied to the global scaling manager position and moved to the United States.

As you can see, what I did set up for after year six happened in year five. Before year five, I wouldn't have been able to move, as my son still needed to be close to my family, but when the opportunity to move to the US came to the table, I was sure that if it was required, I would be able to travel, and he would be okay. As of now, hasn't even been required, as my parents are retired and they come to stay with us when I need to travel for business.

As you can see, when you define what you are willing and what you are not willing to do, your focus takes you through a process of getting things done even before you planned them.

I am already in the process of defining what my next exciting step is in my career, that will keep contributing to my life vision.

If you feel more comfortable defining more specific goals from years one to year ten, please go ahead and define them. If that's the case, I do recommend that you use the S.M.A.R.T goals process, still following the 1/5/10 outline.

For your reference, S.M.A.R.T. goals stand for:

- Specific: What is the desired job, which are the requirements, what benefits do you want, etc.? Be as specific as possible.
- Measurable: How can you quantify by indicators or description the goal completion or progress?
- Achievable: What training is required or who do you need to contact to help you move forward? Is there any training required?
- Relevant: Is the goal in alignment with your life vision and your values? How does this goal play into your journey?
- Timely: What is the deadline? Ensure it is realistic.

In my case, based on my high-level priorities for the 1/5/10, I decided to document three goals for 2012.

By the end of 2012 (Timeframe):

1. Document team development plans. (Specific)
   Achievable and relevant: have had the regional director and team support. Achievable as I have

implemented my 1/5/10 and didn't require any additional training, but the process itself was relevant to my life vision and mission. Measurement: Plans in place—Done.

2. Cover the regional director position during his vacations (Specific)

Achievable and relevant: Was discussed with the regional director beforehand and that coverage supported the objective of strengthening the regional network. Measurement: Coverage done.

3. Execute strengthening my network map. (Specific)

Achievable and relevant: Ensured to establish the connections identified in the network mapping and engage in new connections. Measurement: Done.

Proceed to fill out your 1/5/10.

Connecting the Dots and Creating Your Career Manifesto

"The best way to predict the future is to create it."
– Abraham Lincoln

You already defined your life vision and mission. You have a map of your career cycles, identified the top three potential jobs you're interested in, identified your values, have your resume and short and long bio, and you have a high-level 1/5/10.

Let's put it all together in your career manifesto. Again, you don't need to share this with anyone, but if you decide to do share it, it may help you with accountability. I recommend that you get an accountability partner, who could be a coworker, any friend, or person you trust, who will, once in a while, check on you and keep you accountable to your path. Ideally you set up checkpoints in your calendar.

Your career manifesto is your commitment to yourself and is something to be recalled any time challenges show up. It will recall your vision. Print it, frame it, and keep it close to you. You can also carry it with you as an electronic version. Review it every year and assess if anything needs to be updated.

So, bring all of yourself to define that commitment. These are the questions that I considered when writing mine:

1. What does this mean to me and how is it aligned with my values and strengths?
2. How might my journey affect others?
3. Where will I see my impact? Is it just in my household, community, country, region, or even the world?
4. Does my journey consider travel to other places?
5. Who will be part of my journey?
6. What actions are required to build that journey?
7. What value do I bring to others?

Here is my commitment:

Karla's Career Manifesto
My career allows me to continuously grow and thrive by connecting, lifting, and being lifted by my journey fellows. When I am at the end of my career and I connect the

dots, I will be sure that I lived a life of meaning and significance. Through my different jobs, I will be able to seize and leverage opportunities, not only for myself and my loved ones, but also for many others in my community, my country, and the world. We grow and unleash our potential together. I nurture and enjoy fulfilling relationships. I connect with people and that allows me to connect with myself.

I learn many new and exciting things that contribute to my growth and pave the way for others.

My career takes me to many exciting and unexpected places that enrich my path, learning from different cultures and people. That journey enriches my diversity of perspective. Through my career, I strengthen my voice and give voice to those that were not present or weren't able to bring their thoughts and ideas to the table. I sponsor and I am sponsored, mentor and I am mentored, coach and I am coached. I stand up for my values of respect, courage, and transparency. I build a meaningful career by collaborating with my journey fellows, creating many solutions for humanity and the planet. I create a feeling of belonging for myself and others. I enjoy the beautiful, inspiring, and satisfactory moments. In difficult times, I reconnect with my essence, my tribe, and my Vision. I ask for help and get help beyond what I require. I live in a nurturing world. I keep myself moving forward. I feel proud of my career footprint in the world.

Chapter 5
Board of Advisors

"A coach is someone who tells you what you don't want to hear, and has you see what you don't want to see, so you can be who you have always known you can be."

– Tom Landry

Our life is a beautiful fabric that shows a picture of the interwoven threads of people. People that come and go, masters that guided us in our journey, consciously or unconsciously, but everyone came to teach us something. We make the choice to pick the learning, claim it as ours in our life, and make a good use of it to contribute to our vision.

What is a Board of Advisors (BOA)?
How many Boards of Advisors do you need?

I was introduced to the concept of a Suite of Advisors by a former boss, Shelly Esque. I appreciate the many things that she shared with us to help us become more aware of different situations, and this is one strategy to grow in our career that she shared. I added some advisors to the table, but it's essential to understand that nobody can deploy a magnificent career alone. We need help, and the help is out there, waiting for us to ask.

A Suite of Advisors is a variety of people you can turn to in different situations. Your advisors should include:

- The Pusher: Someone who encourages you to take the action that's in your best interest, even if it's something you don't want to do.
- The Cheerleader: A person who encourages you and gives you moral support.
- The Strategist: A friend or colleague you can pose a challenge to. They will help you talk through it and navigate solutions.
- The Scolder: Someone who can give you honest feedback in a compassionate way.

In my case, I call them a *Board* of Advisors because of the impact that I experienced from their advice in my life. I added some other roles to the list and actually, this is organic, and you can pick and choose different moments to consult with two or more of them. You will get different perspectives and have your own enriched by them. As multidimensional beings, it is helpful to have a BOA for each one of your main dimensions. In my case, I have my BOA for work and at least four more: spiritual matters, family support, physical exercise, meditation practices, and some overlaps. This doesn't require a formal approach, but it is helpful to be aware and conscious of who is in your BOA.

These are the ones that I added to the list:

- The Coach: That person that will ask meaningful questions to help you find the answers that you may need in specific situations. We all have all the answers inside, but there may be times that we need to engage in a conversation to bring those answers out.
- The Mentor: Someone that is a content expert on a specific field or topic who you can connect to get guidance from their expertise.
- The Sponsor: The person that will talk to your strengths when you are not in the conference room. This is the person that supports your career and can see your potential beyond what others see.
- The Inspirator: Those leaders that we observe and are our inspiration to become the best version of ourselves.
- The Circle of Trust: The small group of family or friends that deeply know you, don't judge you, and will be there to support you when you need them.

In life and our careers, we need to have one thing clear: WE ARE NOT ALONE, but we need to ask for help. There are people that expect others to read their minds and know what they need, and sometimes they even create stories in their heads thinking that someone doesn't help for one reason or another, when really the only reason is simple: we don't read minds and although there are many empaths on the planet that know and can read when someone needs help, this is not the majority of people. You need to clearly understand yourself and your needs to be able to clearly articulate the required help.

In Latino culture, we tend to go around and around, taking time to get to the point, and what happens is that sometimes we get people confused because we are not asking directly for what we need. Life is not happening *to* you, life is happening *for* you, but you need to take ownership and be accountable. Remember about the observer. Look at the observer as your best friend who can make the calls when you are not getting the help that you need.

We need to be clear that not everyone will like us, and that is okay. Fortunately, we have the freedom to choose our tribe, but watch out: usually our tribe is filled with people that are similar to us, and if we purposely make an effort to bring different perspectives, it will be easier for us to learn, unlearn, understand, and maneuver our journey. Also, the people that you choose may not be interested in being part of your BOA, and that is okay. Show appreciation for their honesty and move on. You don't need to tell people that you are setting up a BOA; this concept is for you to have clarity of who is part of your life and what roles they are playing. There maybe even be people that show you what you don't want to do, so just by looking at their behaviors and putting them in perspective, you can confirm the coherence that you want in your life.

For different situations in life, we need different BOAs, or the same BOA integrated into sub-teams by topic, getting their fresh view and perspective.

Who is part of my current BOA and how do they contribute to my journey?

Now take a look and make a list of the BOA members in your current situation. How are they contributing to your journey? There may be people that play more than one role in your life, or more than one person in a role, and that is okay. For example, you may call a mentor for a specific topic and another one for a different topic. The importance of this is to understand who your tribe is.

Please grab your workbook or a paper and place a name next to each BOA role. If at this moment you are missing one, don't worry. Take your time and build a connection with people that can play those roles in your near future in order to advance your career. Remember, we don't grow alone.

- The Pusher: Someone who encourages you to take the action that's in your best interest, even if it's something you don't want to do. _____
- The Cheerleader: A person who encourages you and gives you moral support. _____
- The Strategist: A friend or colleague that you can pose a challenge to. They will help you talk through it and navigate solutions. _____

- The Scolder: Someone who can give you honest feedback in a compassionate way. _____

- The Coach: That person that will ask meaningful questions to help you find you answers you may need in specific situations. We all have all the answers inside of us, but there may be times that we need to engage in a conversation to bring those answers out. _____, _____, _____.

- The Mentor: Someone who is a content expert in a specific field or topic who you can connect to get guidance from their expertise. _____, _____, _____.

- The Sponsor: The person that will talk to your strengths when you are not in the conference room. This is the person that supports your career and can see your potential beyond what others see. _____, _____, _____.

- The Inspirator: Those leaders that we observe who are our inspiration to become the best version of ourselves. _____, _____, _____.

- The Circle of Trust: The small group of family or friends that deeply know you, don't judge you, and will be there to support you when you need them. _____, _____, _____ , _____, _____, _____.

A Story: How Shirlene Embraced her Managers as Part of Her BOA to Evolve

Shirlene from Costa Rica started her professional career in 2004 as a student worker and later that year was hired as a trade analyst. In 2012 she assumed a supervisory responsibility as a customs classification supervisor.

In 2015, she became the team manager and landed another global process, which transformed the team into a trade hub that provided global services. Now, this team is part of the global trade facilitation team, and Shirlene is one of the team's four trade global facilitation managers.

Leveraging One of Her BOA Members to Craft Her Own Story

One of her former managers shared with her that she thought she was like a little newly born turtle getting to the ocean. She embraced that comment and interpreted it as follows:

- Newly born turtle: just graduated
- Walking on the beach: walking into her new job
- The ocean: the company: the world

Under that concept, Shirlene saw herself as a little self-confident turtle that knows where she is going, with defined priorities, facing her fears.

Nowadays, Shirlene perceives herself as a grown turtle that has a family and is learning from all of her efforts in the big ocean, conquering her own happiness. As the ocean is huge, she keeps growing professionally and personally, creating the best version of herself and putting everything she has learned to work in the service of others.

Her passions are:

- Feeling peace and happiness
- Practicing compassion with herself and others
- Enjoying optimal health
- Enjoying everything she does
- Unleashing the best version of herself

Personal Challenges and How She Faced Them:

Feeling of inadequacy: When she started to work in a multinational company, she felt inadequate, as everyone spoke English fluently, and she was just starting to learn. Being part of meetings and activities where most people were speaking in a language that she had not mastered was difficult, and she sometimes felt overwhelmed and concerned. She decided to overcome that with classes and getting herself out of her comfort zone with constant practice. It was not easy, and many times it was very uncomfortable to face her own fear of feeling inadequate. She also mentioned that she got support from her amazing network of support and her husband became her main cheerleader in her BOA, always providing positive reinforcement. Her manager at that point was the pusher and sponsor, always next to her ensuring that she got the messages and finding opportunities for her to keep growing. She reports that the feeling of inadequacy is something that has come up many times in her life since she was a child, mainly when she was doing something new, getting out of her comfort zone. When she does not master a topic/area, or when she needs to open herself to others (as she is an introvert and that is hard), she makes the extra effort to keep growing.

Shirlene considers this as a work in progress, taking control over that voice in her head that is trying to keep her safe, acknowledging the feeling but taking ownership and acting in a different place. She states, "We always have to move forward and if we make a mistake, learn from it. This is something I always try to remind myself."

Changes: early in her career when she faced her first management change, it was hard. The new manager was very different, and she didn't feel well working with her. It was difficult for months, until she learned that she needed to change the strategy. She made a list of all of the things that she didn't like and next to them listed what she thought was under her control to change. She made the changes accordingly and the relationship improved to the point that she became her manager's right hand.

She states, "Changes will always come, we just have to be flexible and resilient."

Confronting people and standing up for herself. Shirlene is working on being mindful and listening to her body and feelings. When she feels that something is not right, she tries to pause and think about what happened, what she feels, what she needs, and what she could request from another person or for herself. Using the non-violent communication structure has been very beneficial for her.

Believing in herself and accepting herself as she is. Shirlene mentions that this is still a struggle sometimes. She is currently tackling this with meditation, mindfulness, and self-compassion.

Who else do I need in my BOA to accelerate the career of my dreams?

Go back to the exercise in Chapter 4 where you identified a list of three new people that you need to add to your network in order to get a faster advance in your career. Think about the role that they could play in your BOA. Do you need to add them? There's no right or wrong answer, just reflect on that and remember not to confuse your BOA with your network. Your BOA is part of your network, but not all of your network members are part of your BOA. Go through all of the BOA roles and, if you are missing names, reflect over the next week on who could be part of your BOA. It's not required that you ask people to engage in it with a specific role; what is required is that you have a clear picture of who is playing that role in your career.

My engagement plan—don't wait until it's too late!

Sometimes we don't take the appropriate time to pause and nurture our network and, when we face a career challenge such as a layoff or restructure, we expect the world to come and save us. That is not how life works, so you need to be proactive and ensure that you have an engagement plan in place. You should be meeting your BOA for at least 15 to 20 minutes on a quarterly basis to keep them updated on how your career plans are moving forward, what help you may need, and to be able to seize opportunities. Hopefully you are able to serve and work on a project with the team that may hold the job of your dreams; otherwise, there is a high likelihood that if there is a job opening and others seize the opportunity before you, they will be the ones getting that job. So, don't wait until the job is opened—offer yourself.

When I was in the finance department and offered myself to support the corporate affairs manager, she got to learn about my work style, my commitment, and the results that she could get from me. Later, when the government affairs position opened, I applied but she already knew my job and what I could get done. Actually, just by being closer to her, I knew what the challenges were and proactively provided a strategy to drive solutions. The role that this person was playing in my life was a mentor role, guiding me through a job that didn't exist when I offered myself to help her.

Later, when she went on maternity leave, I covered her position and the general manager became my pusher and sponsor. How did that happen? As I was covering her position, he learned about my commitment and results. When my boss announced that she was leaving, I wasn't planning to apply to the position because I didn't feel ready, but he pushed me to apply, telling me that the worst thing that could happen would be that I learned in the interview what the skills were that I needed to get the job—but there was also the possibility that I would get the position. In addition to being my pusher, he became my sponsor, as he provided very positive feedback to the other members of the interview panel and I got the job.

Set up your engagement plan to proactively engage your BOA members, setting up at least fifteen minutes with them on a quarterly basis. There may be members that need more frequency, and others may need less.

Don't forget to always show gratitude for the time, wisdom, and value added that your BOA brings to your career and life. Send a quick note updating them on how you are doing and moving forward. You need to keep nurturing the relationships. Don't forget: "No man will make a great leader who wants to do it all himself or get all the credit for doing it." – Andrew Carnegie

Map the BOA of Your 1/5/10—Define who can help you reach your 1/5/10 goals.

Now that you have a plan in place, take a second look at your 1/5/10 and double-check if you are missing anyone. If you are, get them into your plan as soon as possible.

Exercise: How does our BOA fit into your new calendar?

Now that you already have a plan in place, what does your new calendar look like? We tend to fill our calendars with many meetings, procrastinating ourselves and our development. Remember your career manifesto and your commitment to yourself and adjust your calendar accordingly.

My recommendation is that out of your total hours each week, you block out 20% of your time for career development, which is not just training but also building and nurturing your network and BOA.

At this point, I would like you to open your calendar for your next week and purposefully mark out time for career development.

> *"The key is not to prioritize what's on your schedule, but to schedule your priorities."*
> **– Stephen Covey**

Exercise: The BOA Picture

I am a visual person and it helps to me when I see pictures. If this is also your case, Google pictures of your BOA and create a visual of them. Invite the new ones to the picture, too. You can simply combine the pictures in a document on your computer, defining each one's role in your life, or you can print, cut, and paste them in your workbook. It's your choice, but it will help you to have a clear image of who is in your BOA and who else should be.

I also create a visual with pictures of leaders that I admire and who inspire me with a quote from them to keep my inspiration flowing.

Chapter 6
THE POWER OF SERVING

*"The best way to find yourself is to
lose yourself in the service of others."*
— **Mahatma Gandhi**

The Two-Way Benefits of Service

A ccording to the Oxford Living Dictionary, "service" is the action of helping or doing work for someone.

As you can see from the definition, at least two people are involved in the equation: yourself and someone else. I say service has two-way benefits because when you give, you receive a lot more than what you are giving, and when you do service from the heart, your self-value increases when you give. Before you can acknowledge that, you need to first be confident of who you are and be open to receive. Life is an endless landscape of opportunities, but you need to be endlessly open to receive all those gifts from life. That's why I say service has two ways, or two sides of the coin. When you feel uncomfortable receiving, it's a flag to take a pause and have a deeper check. I find this very common in my Latino culture, especially for women, because we are taught to give and put ourselves last on the list of receiving.

If you feel uneasy when others give to you, I will share with you a practice that has helped me and many other people in the process of unleashing the best version of a person. That technique is called Ho'oponopono. It's an ancient Hawaiian practice for healing. In this case we will heal our inner child. Why? Because as adults we show up to the world with all that we've learned from our childhood, our confidence and our challenges. Parents played a big role in our childhood, as we looked at them to learn how to behave and receive love and appreciation. In that quest, seeking love and affirmation, some of us learned that when we gave, we received positive reinforcement and, in some cases, put our desires and wishes at the end of our priorities list, since our first priority is to feel loved and belong and that required us to please others. If this resonates with you, practice Ho'oponopono for at least 21 days. This is a powerful tool that can help us to show up in the world with confidence and, most importantly, in our true essence.

If you are on the other side of the spectrum of giving, and perceive yourself as or consistently get the feedback that you are needy, jealous, or even competitive (as sometimes competitive people are on this side of the spectrum and confuse needy with competitive), the question to clarify is why? Why am I so competitive? If it is because you find yourself wanting to be in the center of others' attention or trying to demonstrate that you are the best, it's probably because you were in a big competition during your childhood for the attention of your parents. It could be that there were many other siblings or that your parents worked long hours and they were absent very often, so you were competing for love and attention. It would be also valuable for you to get into the Ho'oponopono healing process. On the other hand, if you are competitive-based, not on comparison against others but because you strive for excellence and you want to be the best version of you, it can be a sane competitive drive, but check it out since sometimes you never feel satisfied with your results and perfectionism backfires your state of peace. I don't mean that you don't look for excellence—we all should look for that—but when our behavior creates a hostile environment for others and ourselves, it's better to check out the roots.

The Ho'oponopono Exercise

It's a Hawaiian practice that translates into English as "edit." According to the ancient Hawaiians, error arises from thoughts that are tainted by painful memories from the past. This practice helps you to release those painful thoughts or errors which can cause imbalance or disease. With this practice, you assume 100% responsibility for the painful situation.

I learned this process as follows: sit comfortably, close your eyes, take three deep breaths in 4x4x4 (inhale counting from 1 to 4, keep the air in your lungs counting from 1 to 4, and release the air slowly to the count of 4), visualize your heart, go there, and when you are there, observe your preferred place. It could be a mountain, beach, river, or any other natural setting. Observe a little kid (yourself as a child) coming to you. Look her in the eyes, hold her hands, ask her what it is that makes her feel _____ (unhappy, sad, uncomfortable, angry, etc.). Let the little child share with you all of her feelings. Hold her in your arms, look her eye to eye and tell her: I am sorry; Forgive me; Thank you; I love you. Repeat this two more times (three in total). Give her a big hug. Take another deep three breaths. Look how she is now leaving relaxed, happy, and in a different state. Open your eyes and enjoy your day. You can use this process whenever you want and especially when you don't feel balanced. As soon as you master it, it becomes very natural and helpful.

I enjoyed this practice because you bring the universal virtues of forgiveness, love, gratitude, and compassion to any difficult situation. You assume the responsibility and you become the change that you want to see.

> *"If you want to solve a problem, no matter what kind of problem, work on yourself."*
> **– Ihaleakala Hew Len**

So, when we are open to give and receive, we are in a great place to find ourselves, when we lose ourselves serving others.

The Value of Service

When we serve from the heart, we are bringing the best version of us to the table. How do you feel after a volunteering activity? Tired but uplifted? Yes and yes. That is because we are here on this journey to help each other to become the best versions of ourselves and, by serving others, we unleash the best version of us. So, I invite you to recall those moments when you felt uplifted and satisfied with a job you had done well. Was that moment a lonely moment? Did you get there alone? Can you recall the faces of all those around you that helped you to get there? That is life. There is an African proverb that says: "If you want to go fast, go alone. If you want to go far, go together."

When we look for a job, we usually look for something that is beyond the monetary pay. We usually look for a job that allow us to do work that matters, work that helps us to leave this world in better shape than when we landed as a newborn on it.

The Virtuous Cycle of Service

> *"The key to growth is the introduction of higher dimensions of consciousness into our awareness."*
> **– Lao Tzu**

The virtuous cycle of service is a loop of actions that provide positive results. I would say that those positive results can be translated as lessons learned or a leap in growth. Although service is not exclusive to working environment (you can apply it to any space in your life), in this book we will focus on service at work. This requires you to be conscious about service, and you may be asking yourself how this connects with your career journey. It connects as follows: you already identified your three potential jobs of your dreams, volunteered yourself to lead a project or contributed in some way to get to know the team, made yourself visible to the team and manager, and demonstrated what you could give to the team. Demonstrate your unique value. You will be adding value to the team and will be getting the value of learning about the organization and its members, so in the end, you can make a better-informed decision about whether you really want to move to that organization.

In many behavioral studies, we learn that women use formal tools to apply for jobs while men use their networks or even conversations in the hall. So, when you contribute to the team where you want to work, you will learn about the job, and by the time the project is finished, you will be sure that it's the job that you want, the boss that you want, and the team and environment where you can thrive.

Can you see now where the virtuous cycle is? You gave value but also received a lot in return, including the possibility to get into the job of your dreams.

That's why I call this conscious service, so you do it intentionally instead of letting the odds take control of your career.

Map of My Current Serving Style and Actions

"The important thing is not to stop questioning.
Curiosity has its own reason for existing."
– Albert Einstein

Now is the time to self-reflect. Open your workbook and answer the following questions:

1. During the last week, did you do something in addition to your regular day-to-day work?
2. Did you allow yourself to serve in any situation? Please describe.
3. How did you feel about the service?
4. If you couldn't serve because you were too busy, on a business trip or any other activity, what is your plan to go and serve to create your new job opportunity? Name three specific actions to move forward.
5. What is your service style? Proactive or reactive? Which one you think would serve you better in your quest?
6. How do you want to implement your virtuous cycle of service?

When you answer those questions and take action, you are moving forward to your next career move, because your answer to the third question provides you with direction to focus your efforts, maybe to that position or to a different direction, depending on your findings in this experience of service. Enjoy and keep moving! Sometimes, we are in difficult situations and are stuck in pain, but the only thing that we can do is to keep moving forward. That way, we better process what is going on. Take a deep breath, stay still, get inside yourself, feel the pain in your body, but after that conscious action, make the decision to quickly move and not stay there for a long period of time, to prevent getting stuck.

My Motto of Service

I want to invite you to write down your motto of service. Connect with your heart and learn what moves you to serve. How does that connect with your vision?

This is my service motto:

"When I connect and serve others I find my essence and feel the joy to get closer to my life vision of living a life of meaning and significance."

– Karla Blanco

Chapter 7

Your Voice, the Ripple Effect of Your Personal Brand

"When you own your voice, you own your power"
– Unknown

Concepts: Your Voice, Ripple Effect, and Personal Brand

- Your voice: the expression of your point of view, your thoughts, and beliefs.
- Ripple effect: the spread of a specific action.
- Personal brand: represents what makes you unique from everyone else.

There are different circumstances in life that strengthen or do not strengthen our voice. Aspects like culture, family rules, community dynamics, and even school teachers have an impact on how comfortable we feel sharing or not sharing our voice. What nobody tells us is that by remaining silent we are hurting ourselves and impacting our confidence. If we live in a nurturing home and community where our opinions and viewpoints are respected, we will probably share them in an easier way, but if we are raised in situations where we are not allowed to talk or share our thoughts, there is a high likelihood that when we grow we will prevent ourselves from sharing, which means that the world will be missing our perspective, our voice. We need to speak up for what we want, what we need, and what we won't tolerate. We need to value ourselves enough to speak our mind. If we don't do that, we will be allowing others to speak on our behalf, and they won't always be representing our truths, because everyone has a different perspective or point of view.

Expressing our beliefs and viewpoints has ripple effects on our lives and contributes to our personal brand, which is what differentiates us from the rest and contributes to show what value we bring to the workplace and other spaces of life.

Elements of Your Voice: What Makes You Unique

*"The most courageous act is still
to think for yourself. Aloud."*
– Coco Channel

Our voice represents our beliefs, our viewpoints, our perspectives, and all that is a mirror of our culture, our family, and the environment that surround us. Although many of us can be part of a culture, from the same country of origin or even coming from the same family, we will all have a unique voice, because we all experience the world in different ways. Three siblings from the same family will have different experiences based on the circumstances that they are each specifically living.

There are different rules in each community and even in the company where we work, and some voices become more influential than others, but the reality is that we need to build a diverse fabric that reflects the diversity of thoughts present, otherwise just one type of voice is represented, excluding the richness of diverse thought and belief, missing important opportunities for us and the company.

It is very common that male voices are more heard in the workplace than female voices, especially when female voices are less than 30% of the population. You need to be conscious when this situation happens and implement your own strategies to ensure your voice is not ignored. There are different strategies for this, such as the "amplification" strategy used by women in the White House during Obama's administration. This consisted of amplifying women's messages through their female fellows, so, if one offered an idea and if it wasn't acknowledged, another woman would repeat it and give her colleague credit for suggesting it.

In my career, two members of my BOA were male leaders in different terms and because they were conscious about the challenges faced by women when they were minorities, they were the ones echoing the ideas for women, amplifying the message and ensuring the credit went to the idea originator and not to the male that picked up the idea and made it his. This doesn't mean that our male fellows are stealing our ideas, it means that we live in a male-dominated environment and this is a male dynamic. They don't wake up thinking, "today I will take Karla's idea," this just flows naturally in their way of doing business. So, while we don't have enough male fellows that ensure that our ideas are amplified and we get the appropriate credit or we become more than 30% in the meetings rooms, we need to use strategies such as speaking with authority, embodying executive presence with vocal conviction, and organizing our thoughts before meetings.

You need to be conscious and aware of the biases present in your workplace and find ways to overcome them. That starts with understanding and acknowledging your own biases and embracing new paradigms and ways to express your voice effectively. Remember to invite and promote more women to the meeting room and get together before meetings to strategize about what you want to get out of each meeting, ensuring that you support each other and amplify the voice of your female fellows.

The Importance of Silence for Listening and Recognizing Your Voice

"Silence is a true friend who never betrays."
— **Confucius**

Silence is a powerful tool that helps us understand from where we come, what has shaped our voice, and how we are showing up every day in the world.

It is our moments of silence when we can reflect and recognize our background and connect the dots of why there are some things that are so important to us and others are just irrelevant, and it's not the same for everyone. Those are moments that give us the gift to reconnect with our essence and our origin. Those moments give us the space to understand why we do or don't stand for our voice. In this time of history where we are overwhelmed with the pace of everything and the huge quantity of demands and expectations, it is extremely important to create and make space for silence.

You need to recognize that not everyone will agree with what you express, but it's key to align what you say with what you think, with your values and vision of life, and that creates a space, a space of coherence, a space to show up as your true self. You create opportunities to create happiness by telling your own and unique truth, because if you don't do it, the contrary will happen: you will become the fake version of someone else and not you. As we talked about before, when we are small kids and we learn that by pleasing others we get attention and affirmation, this can lead us to show up in the world in a version that in the long run creates frustration for us and doesn't lead us to get surrounded by the people that can help us to keep growing or to get the opportunities to connect with our passion.

Include a practice, which could be meditation, a walk, a visit to a park, a mountain, or a lake, or go to the beach and observe the ocean in silence and answer the following questions in your workbook:

1. How am I showing up to the world? Do I speak to my truth? To my essence? Or am I pleasing others?
2. If I were not judged, what would my truth be, the one that comes from my heart and is aligned with my values and life vision?
3. How have my origin, culture, and family background impacted my voice?
4. Where are those places where I can share my voice?
5. Am I willing to stand up for myself and share my thoughts?
6. Am I willing to ask for what I need? What I want?
7. If I had the power to change the world and bring peace and equality to every human on earth, what would my message be?
8. What do I need to do to be able to bring my truth through my voice to the world?

Let those answers rest in silence for one week and come back to them. Would you adjust or change anything?

Awareness and Consistency in Your Voice

"There is a voice that doesn't use words. Listen"

– Rumi

After answering those questions, you will become more aware and conscious of how you are showing up to the world. Is that voice showing your full potential and helping you to get where you want to be?

Although there will be people that will feel uncomfortable with your voice, the right ones will get close to you and you will connect with the opportunities that will really allow you to unleash your full potential and get closer to your vision.

Walk your talk and be consistent with your message. Show up to your values and true self. That is the biggest gift that you can bring to the planet, as there is no one else that has your exact perspective, no one else that has gone through your journey. The world needs you!

I know that you won't have the same conversations with your family, with your friends, and at work, as those are probably different groups of people, but when you are able to see yourself consistently in all groups showing up respecting your thoughts and consistently talking and directing your actions based on your values, you've made it! You are showing up with consistency. There are many people that state, "I am who I am." But when you do a next level of observation, you can notice that consistency is missing or, even worse, that these people have a different behavior with different groups of people. For example, there are some that please high levels of leadership and don't apply the same level of respect to their coworkers or even people that have different "truths" about the same topic, depending on who is in front of them. Reality is that truth will always prevail and for those that don't live to it, there is a longer path to get where they want to be, because life will bring all the required lessons to ensure that we talk to our truth and show up feeling comfortable in our own skin.

Personal Brand: 360 Exercise

"All of us need to understand the importance of branding. We are CEOs of our own companies: Me Inc. To be in business today, our most important job is to be head marketer for the brand called You."
– Tom Peters

Your personal brand is a representation of your identity and it's impacted by how you communicate, engage, dress, and show up. Your walking the talk is part of your brand, but also your voice, your strengths, your values, and passions. All that together creates your brand.

It's a perception from others about you. We always create in our mind a first perception of people, based on our biases and stereotypes learned from our families, own community, and the environment where we grew up. Ideally, we wouldn't make all those assumptions, but it is natural and it's what happens. Besides that perception, we carry our own perception of how others perceive us and it not always is aligned. That's why it is valuable to perform a 360 exercise with at least five people from different backgrounds that interact with us. We called it "360" because ideally, these are people from completely different spaces in our lives; for example, the boss, a coworker, a customer, and/or a partner, among others. Pick not only from your day-to-day, but also if you are part of a chamber or any social group that has a relationship with your job, go and grab that feedback. That helps us to have a clear view on how we are showing up and to make any required adjustments towards the best version of ourselves.

Set up a 15-minute conversation with the identified five people (or more), explaining that you are making your personal brand assessment and that you would like to get their feedback.

Before you start having those discussions, define what your strengths, your values, and your passions are. Write down in your workbook your one minute and three-minute elevator pitch, explaining who you are and what you do. Connect your strengths, values, and passions in your pitch.

Meet with the people that will provide feedback to you. Share with them your one minute and three-minute elevator pitch, as you want to get as much feedback as possible from them.

Ask them to share with you what their perceptions are their perception are about you as a professional. Ask for a specific description and take notes. That should take no more than 15 minutes of conversation. Reply to them, reflecting what you heard from them, and get confirmation. If there is a gap and they are not perceiving anything that is important for you, bring that to the table and have another 15 minute discussion. At the end of the 15 minutes with each of the five people, you will have consistency on how others are perceiving your personal brand.

Hopefully that perception is aligned with what you want to project to the world. If it is not aligned, you can make the required adjustments, checking on your voice, your delivery, and how you are walking your talk.

You need to ensure that you are sharing with the world what you want the world to perceive from you and remember that it is reflected in how and what you communicate, how you dress, and how you consistently show up. If you keep that consistently, people know what to expect from you and that strengthens your brand, because consistency increases trust.

Coherence: Your Voice + Your Actions = Your BRAND

The coherence between your voice and your actions reflects your brand. If you live in coherence, the feedback gathered in the previous section is consistent with your perception of your brand and what you want the world to know about you. This is brand ideal state.

Exercise Your Brand Today

Once you have clear what your brand is and what you want the world to remember about you, it's time to proceed and clearly articulate the elevator pitch, which will help you to consistently position yourself, your strengths, and your aspirations.

Usually we don't give a lot of thought to how we introduce ourselves, and I would like you to think as if you were introducing a third party, your best friend, or a person that you admire a lot.

Understand that getting prepared sets you in a better position to create that first positive perception of people. You share who you are, what you do (including impact), and what you want to do, in a very short way, creating interest for the other person to want to get to know more about you.

Do your homework and create at least three versions of your pitch that will talk to specific audiences, because you need to specialize your pitch to your audience.

Let's work on your thirty second elevator pitch. Open your workbook. You can follow the template below or you can create your own, ensuring that you adjust it to your audience and don't forget to mention your impact. Go for it!

My name is _____ I've been working in _____ company for more than _____ years. My passion is to _____ (add passion and strengths) in order to _____ (share the impact that you want to create) as I was able to _____ (sharing some of your previous results, numbers, and indicators of improvement creates a stronger impact).

The three key elements that can't be missing are: 1. Name and current position 2. Experience or area of expertise 3. Your impact in numbers (for example, savings, cost avoidance, percentage of improvement, or any other indicator that showcases that impact).

Examples:

- Brighid Smith

    My name is Brighid Smith. I've been working at Unlock Your Potential Inc. for more than five years. My passion is to consolidate financial data, as I love financial analysis and all the details that can help companies make better decisions. I was able to reduce more than $100M in product cost last year by comparing some costs of importing products versus buying them locally.

What does this tell you about Brighid?

She is a financial analyst. She loves data analysis and one of her strengths is probably attention to detail. I perceive that she enjoys process improvement, as she mentioned how her passion for data consolidation can help companies make better decisions. Based on her example of last year's analysis that led to an important cost saving for the company, I perceive that she may be a proactive person.

By now, I want to know more about her other examples.

- Clare Sullivan

My name is Clare Sullivan. I've been working with Cloud Designs for three years. I am a web designer. In those three years, I've been able to tap into my passion to create the top two customers' brands, connecting them to their mission and positioning them in the market as innovative brands. Design is a way to express ideas and messages. I see my footprint on every new design or on the refresh of old ones.

What does this tell you about Clare?

She is a creative web designer that instills passion for innovation and translation of messages and ideas to images. I am looking forward to seeing her designs.

- Anne Walsh

     My name is Anne Walsh and I own a coaching company called Dream Jobs. I've been in the market for almost a decade and there have been more than 1,000 lives transformed by connecting them with our coaches. One of my passions is to see people thrive after going through our services.

     What does this tell you about Anne?

     Anne is an entrepreneur that is passionate about transforming people's lives through her company services. I am ready to learn about her company's services to unlock my full potential.

Remember to make this your homework and adjust your elevator pitch to the audience that you are interacting with. I recommend you practice with a friend or any member of your BOA until you feel comfortable and your pitch flows naturally.

Exercise: The Voice of Your 1/5/10 Brand

Now let's bring out your 1/5/10 and get a closer look. Is it aligned with your brand? Hopefully it is consistent. If you find any tune up opportunities, go for it! Ensure that you are the storyteller of what you want, and that your strengths are highlighted and present on people's minds.

Your BOA Strengthens Your BRAND

Your Board of Advisors are consciously or unconsciously strengthening your brand. They are the ones that will talk about you when you are not in the conference room. If you include them in your 360 personal brand assessment, you not only get their feedback, but you can also reinforce to them the messages that you want to portray.

Don't forget to nurture your network and BOA. Take ownership of your career.

> *"You don't need to be right,*
> *but you need to move forward."*
> **– Gloria Mayfield Banks**

The Ripple Effect: Stand Up and Share

The ripple effect of the results of a specific action. Your journey inside has just started but I want you to always remember that hope is the wish for something to happen, faith is believing that it will happen, but courage is making it happen. You are not here to play small, you are here to play big and remind yourself of all the gifts that were given to you and how you use them not only for yourself and your loved ones, but also to impact the lives of others. Courage sets you up for confidence and confidence leads you to choice.

The journey is not easy, but when you are bringing your true self consistently and your message and actions are having those ripple effects, you start seeing how your beautiful footprint is making a difference, how you are creating that life of significance. A life that brings lights and shadows, but a life that is unique and has its own impact to many in its own way, because you bring your unique perspective.

Be brave, be willing to show up, and demonstrate the value that you can add.

Fernanda from Brazil stands up and calls our attention to two concerns that we need to address regarding our gender equality journey. Reflecting on her career, she expressed that on our way to reach gender equality there should be two specific priorities in the transformation:

- Men and women's contributions should be valued equally in the same conditions. Her observation is that women need to work harder than men to be valued, respected, and move up the leadership ladder. She would like more gender consciousness to purposefully solve those differences, not only for women but for all minorities. She shows up to the world working to create opportunities for underrepresented minorities.

- Encourage sorority and eliminate the queen bee paradigm. She invites women to become more aware of their behaviors since in many cases, according to her experience, they were the ones setting the roadblocks for her. Sometimes when women access leadership positions and are unconscious of their behaviors, instead of giving a hand to others that come behind, they put up challenges and make it more difficult for them. A positive example and what Fernanda would like to see more present in the workplace is sorority, when women learn about their own biases, support each other, and become agents of change, paving the path for their female fellows. One of her proudest experiences was creating opportunities for girls to engage in careers in science, technology, and math.

She states that the positive aspect of those experiences is that those challenges made her stronger and more aware so that she could support other women in situations of injustice or lack of opportunity. She never gives up!

In her words:

"I learned that woman, wife, mother, and professional are the same person and that we can and should fail like any human being. When I understood and accepted this, I got the ability to think with confidence that I'll always be ready and open for the next challenge."

Allowing us to fail, learn, and keep it up gives us strength to keep moving forward.

Chapter 8

THE WORLD NEEDS YOU! RELEASE THE BEST VERSION OF YOU

"What do you do, speaks so loudly …
I cannot hear what you say."
– Ralph Waldo Emerson

To be able to release the best version of you, it's essential that you learn about yourself in a profound way and explore your life from different angles, but it's more important that you are able to see how you behave and react every day to different circumstances. What are those traits that are so present in you?

Let's talk about you, your: values, strengths, passions, emotions … anything else?

When was the last time that you stopped and reflected on those? I hope that it was recently. If not, it's important to recall that if you've been focusing on your job, your family, friends, and many other "priorities" and not that much on yourself, the reflection point is NOW.

Why you do that? Is this an obvious question with an obvious answer? Does the answer go like this?

Because …

1.   … My family is *first*.
2.   … My job is a *top* priority.
3.   … My friends deserve *all* my attention and support.

All that is good, but what about you? Are you in good alignment? In your thoughts, emotions, passions, values, job, and your life in general, do you feel all are aligned? When you see your week backwards, do you close the week thinking: I am happy and satisfied? If that's the case, there is a high likelihood that everyone around you will be better too, just because you will be able to give the best of you, not a tired and frustrated version of you. Sometimes we just throw ourselves into a vicious cycle of giving and giving without thinking about recharging and reinvigorating ourselves. Then what follows is that we get frustrated, angry, or just uncomfortable not being able to give our loved ones what they deserve.

Remember when we talked about our childhood and how we learned to please everyone around us to get affirmation and love? When we are growing, that behavior shows up and, responding to many external demands from others, we just stop paying attention to ourselves or don't even know what we want. We will explore more about you and your essence, because those insights will enable you to move forward with intent and impact.

Let's take a look inside. We will be discussing our values, strengths, passions, and emotions, but there are many other important factors that create our identity and how we show up every day. There is cultural heritage but also our family footprint. There is our environment, community, region, and even the side of the world where we were born and raised (East, West, North and South). There are so many factors that influence us in a unique way. The people that influenced us when we were growing, like school teachers and our friends, all of that has an impact on how we behave. As you can see, we are a complex compound of experiences and heritage and it's our decision to make a change and leave behind the behaviors that are not serving to our life vision. Life doesn't happen to us, it happens for us … for us to learn and grow.

We need to get in touch to things that bring the best out of us and manage what doesn't bring our best version. That's why this book is about inviting awareness to the table, close to us, connecting with yourself, and action to reach your life vision.

In this section, we will be focusing on four areas, but I need you to go deeper and reflect on your family, community, and all that surrounds you and may have had an influence on you.

This is your exercise and the purpose is to bring awareness, take full ownership, and have an intentional approach. Please pick the items from each chart that have an immediate connection with you. I placed a list after each category, but you can add all that you want.

After that first selection, pick the top ten that really describe you and finally pick the top five. Keep that list with you and, at the end of the process, run a description of who you are using the identified values, passions, strengths, and emotions. Compare those with your personal brand and your elevator pitch. Do you find consistency? How does everything tie together?

VALUES:
The principles and standards that guide your life.

VALUES						
Authenticity	Ambition	Accountability	Achievement	Adventure	Authority	Autonomy
Awareness	Balance	Beauty	Bravery	Boldness	Candor	Challenge
Citizenship	Collaboration	Comfort	Commitment	Compassion	Confidence	Consciousness
Control	Courage	Creativity	Curiosity	Dedication	Determination	Discovery
Diversity	Drive	Effectiveness	Empathy	Empowerment	Enjoyment	Equality
Ethical	Excellence	Discipline	Fairness	Faith	Fame	Fearless
Flexibility	Freedom	Friendship	Foresight	Growth	Happiness	Harmony
Honesty	Humor	Inclusion	Influence	Independence	Innovation	Inquisitive
Integrity	Justice	Kindness	Knowledge	Leadership	Learning	Love
Loyalty	Openness	Optimism	Passion	Peace	Pleasure	Poise
Popularity	Professionalism	Quality	Realistic	Recognition	Reflective	Religion
Reputation	Respect	Responsibility	Results Oriented	Risk	Security	Selfless
Service	Spirituality	Security	Self-Respect	Stability	Status	Success
Teamwork	Tolerance	Transparency	Trustworthiness	Vision	Wealth	Wisdom

STRENGTHS:
The qualities that allow someone to deal with problems or situations in a determined and effective way.

STRENGTHS				
Accountable	Analytical	Business Acumen	Coach	Collaboration
Communication (written and verbal)	Composure	Computer/Tech literacy	Consistency	Critical thinking
Creative	Data Analysis	Detail-oriented	Discipline	Drive
Efficiency	Empathy	Energized	Focus	Flexible/Adaptable
Growth mindset	Initiative	Interpersonal	Leadership	Mentor
Negotiation	Network	People oriented	Organize, plan, and prioritize work	Results-Driven
Quick learner	Resilience	Resourceful	Responsible	Tolerance
Self Awareness	Story telling	Strategy	Strong work ethic	Visionary

PASSIONS:

The activities, situations, or objects that produce an intense desire or enthusiasm. Usually hobbies are driven by passions, but we don't necessarily have a hobby for all our passions.

PASSIONS				
Learning	Teaching	Scuba Diving	Flying	Travel
Collecting Antiques	Painting	Cooking	Dancing	Sports
Vehicle restoration	Art Collection	Vintage cars	Fishing	Navigation
Art Crafts	Photography	Reading	Movies	Wine Tasting
Add all yours....				

EMOTIONS:

The state of mind deriving from one's circumstances, mood, or relationships with others, typically accompanied by physiological and behavioral changes in the body. Emotions and feelings are different and actually they take place in different parts of the brain. Emotion is that first reaction and feeling is how the emotion evolves in our mind, how we experience it.

EMOTIONS					
Admiration	Anxiety	Attraction	Sadness	Shock	Surprise
Boredom	Contempt	Delight	Optimism	Pride	Relief
Disgust	Doubt	Ecstasy	Irritation	Isolation	Joy
Enjoyment	Enthusiasm	Envy	Embarrasment	Happiness	Humility

Antonio Damasio, Professor of Neuroscience, Psychology, and Philosophy at the University of Southern California and head of the Brain and Creativity Institute, has shown that emotions play a central role in social cognition and decision-making. Find below some of his statements that I found helpful to clarify the role of emotions on our lives:

- "Feelings are mental experiences of body states, which arise as the brain interprets emotions, themselves physical states arising from the body's responses to external stimuli. (The order of such event is: I am threatened, experience fear and feel horror.)"
- "We are not thinking machines that feel; rather, we are feeling machines that think."
- "Rather than being a luxury, emotions are a very intelligent way of driving an organism toward certain outcomes. "
- "When we talk about emotion, we really talk about a collection of behaviors that are produced by the brain. You can look at a person in the throes of an emotion and observe changes in the face, in the body posture, in the coloration of the skin and so on."
- "… I sense that stepping into the light is also a powerful metaphor for consciousness, for the birth of the knowing mind, for the simple and yet momentous coming of the sense of self into the world of the mental."

Now that you have in front of you, in your table, the values, strengths, passions, emotions, and any other behavior that you can highlight as results of influences when you were growing up, let's paint the picture of who you are TODAY.

I will use myself as example to make the points clear.

Karla Blanco
Strengths: Empathy, Includer, Learner,
Responsibility, Harmony.

Values: Commitment, Collaboration,
Courage, Boldness/transparency, Respect.
Passions: My son, My loved ones, Reading, Meditation,
Making a positive footprint on people's lives.
Emotions: Gratitude, Happiness, Joy, Isolation, Fear.

Karla is a daughter, mom, sister, niece, and friend that values bold and transparent people and shows up with courage, respect, and commitment. She has a positive outlook on life, showcasing joy, gratitude, and happiness as she moves on her day-to-day. As a human being there are things that she works on a day-to-day basis to keep improving, such as isolation and fear. She is an introvert and during her childhood used to have just a few close friends, making isolation very present in her life. She acknowledges that if she is able to connect with and embrace a diverse group of human beings, she can enrich her life perspective. Once she identified isolation and fears as part of her emotions, she has been intentionally getting out of her comfort zone. Her strengths include: empathy, includer, learner, responsibility, and harmony. She is a compassionate person that always make an effort to put herself at the feet of her counterparts, understanding that everyone has a specific journey and a reason to behave in one way or another.

Her preferred role in life is being a mom. She loves spending time with her loved ones but has many other passions and interests such as reading, meditation, and leaving a positive footprint on people's lives. She also enjoys dancing and scuba diving. In her journey of dance, she became a teacher with students from 12 to 60 years old, appreciating the power of transformation that dance creates in women as they let themselves bring their full self, expressed in the art of dance.

Her passion for leaving a positive footprint on people's lives led her to engage in programs that have a ripple effect on many other women, even creating a program called "I am the change," honoring Gandhi's quote, "Be the change you wish to see in the world." Another collateral of that passion is this book, which she hopes will help many other women get a fast track in their career growth by unleashing their potential and showing up in the world as the best version of themselves.

That is Karla in essence today, which is present in many other different roles that I play in life. One of those is the professional life. I emphasize TODAY, as building the best version of ourselves is a continuous journey that leads us to beautiful and challenging moments in life. Life is not a linear selection of good or bad moments, life is a compound of different moments that bring different flavors and colors and that allows us to go deep to learn more and more about ourselves, but it is our responsibility and what we do with that learning is our decision. We can keep a scarcity mindset, complaining and feeling sorrow about everything, looking as it life was happening *to* us, or we can choose the growth mindset and expand our wings and footprint, appreciating that life is actually happening *for* us. In my case, I constantly invite awareness to my table and leverage on my journey fellows' feedback to grow together. It is said that it takes a village to raise a kid, but I would say that it takes a world to grow ourselves, as if we connect with the deep essence of all our life traveler fellows, we not only enrich our life with their different perspectives but we evolve faster. This doesn't mean that we will leave our essence behind, because actually that essence is what makes you unique (plus all the other life experiences), but we get out of our bubble and get a bigger picture.

Share Who You Are in Your Professional Role: Let's Build Your Bio and Resume

The bio and resume are important documents that you should be updating at least once a year to use for speakerships or any events that you are invited to—even for your LinkedIn, Facebook, or other social media accounts. Remember that you want consistency of your brand! Be sure that even if, in your mind, Facebook is just for personal purposes, it is really hard to keep the line, as there will be close friends of yours that are from work and recruiters that look on social media to identify candidates.

Remember that in this book, I am sharing my experiences and perspective, so I summarized what works for me, sharing the advice of experts that have been part of my journey. If for any reason you don't resonate with the examples below, you can Google it and will find many examples of bios and resumes. You can even buy beautiful templates, but even more important than the template is what you include there, so, take your time, bring all your accomplishments, strengths and interesting facts to this creative process, and show the world who you are.

Building Your Bio

A biography is the summary of key highlights of someone's, mainly professional life written in a third person voice. It can be a short version. In that case, it can be just few sentences forming a paragraph, a maximum of two paragraphs, with a total number of 100 to 200 words. The long version can be from 300 to 500 words. This is based on my experience sending my bio for different events and also introducing people. For any speakership, I would recommend sending the short bio and aligning with the event coordinator if more info is required. Sometimes people send long stories that are not relevant for the event and if the event coordinator is not cautious enough and cuts it and tries to balance it in relation with other presenters, it can become very light for the audience and you will miss the opportunity of being introduced with impact. Remember that everything you do or don't do is part of your personal brand, bringing the uniqueness of you to life.

It's very important to have clear to where and why are you sending your bio, so you expand on the areas of the audience's interest or eliminate those that are not relevant for the specific audience or objective. It is very important to keep the short and long versions updated with you. Update them at least once a year.

Consider having ready the following information to build your bio:

1. What are my major professional achievements? List them and pick the most impactful ones.
2. Your educational background, awards, and recognitions.
3. Key contributions of impact and any community leadership roles.

4. Depending on the event, it would be valuable to add your strengths and passions.

Here are my short and long versions of my bio as example.

Bio (Short Version)

Karla is an Aspen Institute Fellow and corporate executive leader with more than 20 years of experience working with a Fortune 100 Corporation. She has gone through many restructuring processes and layouts. Her positive outlook on life and ownership of her growth process has allowed her to work out her meaningful career and has helped her mentees to unlock their potential to enjoy meaningful careers and fulfilling lives by unleashing the best version of them.

Bio (Long Version)

Karla Blanco is a corporate executive leader with more than 20 years of experience working with a Fortune 100 Corporation. She is an Aspen Fellow from the Central America Leaders Initiative (CALI), focusing on a program from Leadership to Significance.

She started as an analyst in the finance department, then moved up the career ladder as manager and regional and global director of the corporate affairs group. She managed the corporation interaction with media, community, government, and other external stakeholders.

She studied customs administration and holds an MBA with international business emphasis.

She represented the corporation in different boards of directors as Industries Chamber, Association of Free Zone Companies, Association of Businesses for Development (CSR). In 2009 she got a recognition from a business newspaper in Costa Rica, "El Financiero," as a country leader. Every year the newspaper recognizes the top 40 country leaders under 40 years old.

She is a certified mentor of Vital Voices in Costa Rica, which is a non-governmental organization (NGO) that identifies, trains, and empowers emerging women leaders and social entrepreneurs around the globe. Vital Voices looks to invest in and bring visibility to extraordinary women around the world by unleashing their leadership potential to transform lives and accelerate peace and prosperity. As part of this association she has been a mentor of a small shop entrepreneur. She has been also driving from her area of responsibility efforts to engage women in science and technology and to create consciousness on the importance of educating girls and women to drive an economic improvement in the country. Due to her leadership, the Vital Voices Costa Rican chapter launched the first group of male mentors at Intel and at a global level to support diversity and inclusion.

She has gone through many restructuring processes and layouts. Her positive outlook on life and ownership of her growth process has allowed her to work out her meaningful career and helped her mentees to unlock their potential to enjoy meaningful careers and fulfilling lives by unleashing the best version of themselves.

Karla enjoys spending time with her son, Andres, her friends, and her family. She has a special passion for the ocean and is a certified scuba diver. Meditation is part of her daily routine but she also enjoys reading and dancing.

The Resume

Your resume shouldn't be more than two pages long and you need to consider that recruiters and managers get many at a time, so they will do a quick scan of your resume. They will get a perception of you from the first half of the first page and maybe move quickly to the end, so be cautious of what you want to include and ensure you create interest so that they want to get to know you better, interview you, and learn more of the value that you can add.

A recommendation would be to include the name of the position that you are interested in below your name, followed by a brief description of who you are in no more than 50 words. This could be your short bio. After that description, you want to add your skills, such as: negotiation, leadership, mentoring, coaching, strategy, product marketing, collaboration, media management, social media, ICT literacy, communications, etc. You need to ensure that what you add as skills is reflected in your accomplishments.

Now, to highlight your main professional accomplishments, you need to pick and choose. You can have a regular timeline of positions nailing down your key accomplishments for each position, or you can decide to do a functional resume, which means that you pick functions that you think would be relevant to the position that you are applying for. For example, you might pick on leadership or marketing as a function to showcase your 3 to 5 main leadership accomplishments. To create a more impactful resume, you need to include indicators, such as percentages of improvement, changes that you led, time and cost savings, etc.

After listing two or three main functions, you can list all of your formal positions including dates, at least years. If you have as many years of experience as me, you don't need to include ALL of your positions, just the most relevant ones. Remember that they will look on the first page first.

Following your formal positions, you should include your education, followed by publications, awards, and recognitions.

Resumes reflect yourself, so there are plenty of ways and alternatives. Pick the one that fits your needs, but ensure that shows consistency and uses powerful words about you. This is not the time to be shy, this is the time to show your full self.

Who will you be in 1/5/10 years?

Bring out your 1/5/10 again. Take a look at it and let's brainstorm what needs to happen in year one to set yourself on the right path for year five and year ten. For example, if you are interested in evolving to a leadership position in the company where you are working now, what would the characteristics be that would be required and built in order to get there? Leverage your BOA, have a conversation with them, and define your path of success.

At this point, you have explored many aspects of your life and you know where you need to focus your efforts. I would like you to take a look to what you defined on your 1/5/10, considering the point that we are discussing. Are you going to keep it as it is or would you like to identify three specific actions that you will be doing to get there? Define in your 1/5/10 one thing that you are doing to get to year five and in year five, define two specific actions that can take you to year ten. That sounds simple, but is powerful. Commit to yourself and move forward in the direction that you have defined. You may have in your mind an idea of what it is that position that you want, but my suggestion is that you shouldn't get attached to a job title, as you don't know what life has prepared for you. It may be something more exciting that you haven't even imagined yet. Life has surprised me in so many beautiful ways just by being open, doing my best, and moving forward with intent and purpose.

We experience many challenges in life. Please write down a list of what would be an obstacle to get you to year five and ten. Pick three. I want you to be aware of and to play with different possible scenarios. Identify the possible obstacle, the scenario of how that could impact what you want or are willing to do in your year five or year ten, and what the solution or alternative could be if that happens. When we have scenarios defined and are prepared, we feel more confident making decisions if those come.

Now that you already identified some of the possible showstoppers, move forward to take a look from a different perspective: the heritage. Analyze which showstoppers or obstacles are based on that. For example, you may see in your parents or ancestors a risk of adverse behavior and identify that as possible root of one of your showstoppers. Another example could be comparing yourself with others. We already talked about how everyone is on a unique journey with unique experiences. Even twins or people from the same family experience life in a different way, so it doesn't make sense to make comparisons which may lead us to a scarcity mindset. If you want to make a comparison, do it with yourself, remember where you were last year and where are you today, compare how you grew and look forward to your future self, how you envision that version of you. I would like to invite you to make a commitment to yourself, take control over those behaviors, and turn them to your advantage. This requires practice. There are behaviors that we know come to surface in specific situations, so pick one and define what would be a behavior that instead of becoming a roadblock could get you faster to where you want to end up. In the example of comparing ourselves with others, the internal dialogue could go like this: "Oh see, she got that promotion that I deserved and was not given to me." That is a scarcity mindset, as you are comparing yourself with someone else that got something that you didn't but you wanted. In a growth mindset position, you catch yourself making the comparison and jump into your self-analysis about why you didn't get that promotion. Ask where you were last year. Did you make contributions that deserve that promotion? Are you performing to that next level? Did you have that conversation with your manager, asking what was required to get to the next level? Did you take actions and proactively check on a quarterly basis how you were advancing and if you were on the right path to potentially get that promotion? If the answers are yes and you didn't get it, it's important to take ownership and have a conversation with your manager about what happened and what was missing that you weren't aware of. This should be a rich conversation to get you moving forward. If the answers are no, take a look at this as an opportunity to take ownership and move differently in the coming year, setting up those discussions and checking on your advancement. Time is priceless. Don't lose it comparing you with others, use it investing in yourself and focusing on your career path.

Define what those required adjustments are and introduce the daily, monthly, and yearly check in, to become aware of how you are evolving. Add it to your calendar. If it's not on your calendar it doesn't exist and it's very possible that you will get into your regular routine and lose your track. Be mindful of your circumstances, learn not to punish yourself. That doesn't move us forward and can delay us getting where we want to be. If you make a mistake, take the lesson learned and move forward. Celebrate your wins, find sources of inspiration, connect with people that uplift you, and keep yourself moving forward.

Living a Life of Consciousness: Release the Best Version of You

> *"Until you make the unconscious conscious,*
> *it will direct your life and you will call it fate."*
> **– Carl Jung**

Everyone is in their own journey and responding to life from their state of consciousness.

You've been exploring your life and have tools to bring conscious to every day and every moment of your life.

Mindfulness is a great tool to keep that awareness present. Some people judge mindfulness as a "weird" practice. I have heard comments such as: "People may lose control of themselves practicing it" or that it's tied to a specific religion, and many other stories around it. Being mindful means being present and conscious. It is easy to find ourselves thinking about past events or about future potential and missing the present moment and all the gifts that come with it.

When you take time to simply consciously breathe, you are bringing more clarity to your present moment because you are oxygenizing your brain and body. Mindfulness allows you to connect with your feelings and body sensations and to clean your thoughts. It provides the space for you to create a more positive outlook and a growth mindset.

I want to invite you to enjoy taking three deep breaths. Inhale, counting from one to four, keeping the air in your lungs another four counts and slowly releasing in another four counts. How do you feel now? This is a practice that you can make wherever you are and helps to bring calm to your body and refocus on the moment.

Life is beautiful but also can bring important challenges, and how we maneuver those challenges will impact the end result.

I want to share Naty's journey of consciousness as a great example of how she turned a challenging relationship with her manager into creating a growth advantage for herself by being conscious and mindful.

Natalia started back in 2013, and by 2015 was already a product development engineer. She took an opportunity in 2017 to cover the community engagement and volunteering manager position, and by the end of that year became a strategic planner. One of her passions is to motivate and inspire others to develop themselves and break stereotypes, especially for women, in order to prevent gender from becoming a roadblock on their growth. That's why she engaged with Vital Voices Global Non-Profit organization.

Her efforts promoting young women engagement in STEM (Science, Technology, Engineering, and Math), were recognized by the International Visitors Leadership program from the US embassy in Costa Rica, which took a group of young women leaders to visit organizations that are focused on driving change.

Another one of her passions is continuous improvement in every activity that she engages in. She is passionate about simplifying things.

When she implements any give-back activity, in the community or in any other space of her life, she shares the best practices in order to ensure that others take advantage of what is already in place and spread the voice.

Becoming mindful and present on her day-to-day helped her to overcome one of her biggest personal challenges, which was to objectivize her emotions, understanding that she is not the emotion. She can feel the emotion but can also take ownership of how she reacts to the emotions. This helps her to become more efficient when difficult situations arrive.

She changed her perspective about problems, understanding that problems are learning opportunities. Her new approach is not to live the problem, but to take a look at it as an observer, understand it, and see possible solutions and how the situation can be changed instead of taking it personally. Her new approach to problem solving has brought to her many recognitions in the workplace.

The third challenge was her perspective that things should be in her own way. Nowadays, opening her mind and heart has enriched her life in many ways. In the past she didn't even consider working in industrial engineering or with people, but opening to the opportunity led her to go deeper and learn more about herself.

In Naty's words, "One of my biggest learnings was that managers and people around me don't define who I am. Asking for help helped me to manage difficult situations. For example, I didn't have the best relationship with my manager, but opening myself and sharing my aspirations with him, led him to help me find my best next job opportunity."

Naty's short but rich experience is an invitation to us to challenge ourselves. To be mindful and value the present moment. To ask for help when needed and to give a hand always to others, so we help each other to keep growing.

Take a chance on you. Become more conscious of how everything takes place in your life and make decisions that have a positive impact and contribute to your journey.

"You miss 100% of the shots you don't take."
— **Wayne Gretzky**

Chapter 9

LIFE HAPPENS. HOW TO RECONNECT WITH YOUR JOURNEY—RESILIENCE

"The greatest glory in living lies not in never falling, but in rising every time we fall."
– Nelson Mandela

In this chapter we acknowledge that even when you have a plan, know yourself very well, and are showing up consistently to the world, there are external challenges and circumstances that can impact your path. So, in this chapter we will talk about the importance of resilience integrated with our life compass and the four universal virtues of gratitude, forgiveness, compassion, and love that can help us keep or get back on track.

Life happens. Why is resilience a powerful tool?

As we talked about before, life is beautiful in its own complexity. It brings us moments of joy and happiness but also difficult moments and challenges. Resilience is our ability to recover quickly from those difficult times.

Maddi and Khoshaba made a 12-year longitudinal study at the University of Chicago. They identified three key beliefs that helped people turned adversity into an advantage:

1. Commitment: led them to strive to be involved in ongoing events, rather than feeling isolated.
2. Control: led them to struggle and try to influence outcomes, rather than lapse into passivity and powerlessness.
3. Challenge: led them to view stress changes, whether positive or negative, as opportunities for new learning.

Those who thrived showed the following attitudes:

- I can influence things, and I do it.
- I can change situations for the better.
- Don't accept events at face value.
- Change is normal and a helpful path to learning and personal transformation.

Those who didn't thrive showed the following attitudes:

- I am at the mercy of the circumstances.
- Prepared for the worst.

- Change is threatening.
- Status quo is normal and change is unusual.
- Life is meaningless.
- Bored with life.

Challenges in life come in many different colors and packages. It's on us how we react and is on us to see them as growth opportunities or to feel powerless and victimized. In our professional life, there may be organizational changes, you may be delighted with your group or boss and due to external conditions, changes may come and suddenly you are in a totally different environment. You may find some toxic non-positive environments. Problems arise in many forms such as: merchandise delays impacting customers, impacting production, or even problems in the community where the company operations can impact the company. If you have the tools to face those challenges, you will overcome them in a healthy way. One of those tools is resiliency.

In the previous chapter, Natalia was an example of moving from reacting to proactively responding to an external stimulus.

People that usually react are almost always ready to fight, flee, or freeze. That shows a disconnect, lack of consciousness, and living on autopilot, lost in emotions and blaming the external world for what happens. There are many circumstances that we can't control, but how we react to them makes a huge difference in the outcome.

Here are some ways to ensure we are strengthening our resilience muscle:

1. Mindfulness and self-awareness. Become your own best friend and keep constant communication with yourself. Be aware of your emotions and how you face the challenges.
2. Identify things that inspire you and bring you positive emotions.
3. Don't isolate yourself. Ensure that you keep your connections flowing and create your circle of support, which is essential to keep perspective. Bring to that circle people that love you but are open to give you compassionate feedback. Assess with them options and alternatives.
4. Keep yourself productive. Identify ways to keep adding value. That provides you the sense of control and moving forward.
5. Get out of your comfort zone. Get out of the house, go and connect with nature and your loved ones.
6. Take care of yourself, keep healthy habits, eat clean, and do exercise.

Exercise

I am strong believer in having potential scenarios thought out, so, when situations come I am ready. Bring your workbook and let's define a scenario that requires your resilience.

1. Define a difficult situation. It could be a challenge that you may be facing now or identify any potential challenge.

2. Think about how you would react, what the emotion would be that you think may come in a moment of a situation like the one described: frustration, anger, sadness, etc. Write down the emotion or emotions.

3. Accept the emotion or emotions without judging it. If you find yourself judging it, take note and analyze from where that judgment comes. Is this from someone else? Try to get back without judging.

4. Take a deep breath, counting from one to four. Keep the breath for four counts. Exhale slowly in four counts. Repeat this process two more times, so you get three deep breaths. It may sound simple but it's powerful.

5. Now feel in your heart a positive emotion like joy, happiness, gratitude, etc.

6. Take another three breaths.

7. Now take a second look at the situation and bring some ideas from your creative self.

And remember: "Kites rise highest against the wind, not with it."
– Winston Churchill.

Courage Sets You Up for Confidence and Confidence Leads You to Choice

Erika from Mexico. She started her career in the government as marketing director for the Cuernavaca Municipality and has spent her last four years with a tech Fortune 100 company. She has deployed her career in the public, private, and academy sectors. She has twice been the head of online and offline communication efforts, strengthening the image and public relations of the Cuernavaca Municipality. She also occupied the same position as the secretary of government at Morelos State. Later was invited to join the tech sector as education and community programs manager.

Erika's passions are cooking and trying new stuff. She loves to help people, spend time with friends, and invite people to her home. She plays with her daughter and teaches her new things and to enjoy the world. She enjoys traveling and discovering new places in the world. She likes to learn about new cultures and meet new people.

Her biggest challenges are life-related. She lost her mom when she was 15, her sister was 11, and her brother seven. This was a very hard hit from life, but she quickly realized that they had two options:

1. Become the "poor" girl that lost her mom and use that excuse the rest or her life, or
2. Stand up and keep moving forward.

As you learned about her, you clearly know what her choice was. She also lost her father the year of her wedding. It was very hard for her to see how his life was fading away due to cancer. For her it was very important to have her father walk next to her the day of her wedding, but that was not possible. Again, life gave her two choices the day of her wedding:

1. Don't enjoy that important day because her parents were not physically there, or

2. Be grateful with life because her two wonderful siblings were there with her, and be grateful for the wonderful guy that she loved and with whom she would share the rest of her life.

Life is not perfect, and many times brings hard challenges, but as Erika shows to us, it's always your choice to keep moving forward, bringing resilience and choosing happiness.

> *"History has shown us that courage can be contagious, and hope can take life of its own."*
> **– Michelle Obama**

Your Life Compass

Besides building and strengthening resilience, having your life compass well-defined will help you to keep out of your path all the noise that comes our way every day. When challenges come and you use resiliency to face them, your life compass is an internal guide which provides direction to your actions. It is the big guide for those core values in your life that are non-negotiable and guide your path. From the values that you identified in Chapter 8, you can identify your life compass is, which values are the guide of your actions, and integrate them into your resiliency strengthening process.

In one of my former teams, there was this amazing professional that was able to keep delivering results despite any circumstances and even big changes that came to us. They didn't stop her. I want to share a little summary of her story with you, as her life compass is what helped her to keep the focus through all the challenges.

Masayo (Maria del Rosario) from Colombia's life compass: "I can reach whatever I want and I keep my focus on creating a positive impact in the lives of people." Her values: courage and drive ("I can reach whatever I want"); compassion and empathy ("keep my focus on creating a positive impact in the lives of people").

She graduated from university the day that the airplane crashed into the twin towers in New York City. A university professor invited her to join her team in the Telecommunications National Planning Office of the government. Later, she moved to the Minister of Telecommunications and worked closely with the vice minister who pushed her to get out of Colombia to get her MBA. Masayo's drive helped her get a scholarship and use all her savings to fly and live in London to improve her English and be able to get to her goal. Her values of compassion and empathy were the roots of her conviction that working with government was the way to impact and change many people's lives. She has courage and drive; the comfort zone is not for her and she is always looking out for what her next step is. She has a can-do attitude and is convinced that she can reach whatever she wants.

Coming back from her MBA, she realized that she could also change the world by engaging with the private sector, that government was not the only option to create a social impact. She embarked on her new phase within a nonprofit organization, which was fundamental for her to value where she was in life. By walking and visiting rural communities, she states that she got the best coffees and most delicious food, food from people that shared with her the only meal that they probably had for the day. Working there got her an invitation to work in a Fortune 100 company, where she says she was able to create different solutions to have a social impact from the private sector. She identifies her key learnings as: if you have the will and commitment you can get whatever you want, and you will learn a lot from the difficult bosses, take those learnings with you. The important thing is to keep the focus. She started out covering just Colombia and later covered many other countries in the region. When the restructuring process arrived, she learned that she was somehow resistant and didn't like the change, but that flexibility and positive outlook are essential to keep moving forward.

After that process, she did explore entrepreneurship, which she didn't enjoy so she embarked on a new journey, changing to a new sector, different than technology but with her life compass clear, a compass that called for the improvement of the lives of many people through her footprint. She mentions that although she was afraid of this new change, she got a vow of trust and is convinced that she will keep growing and supporting the company's evolution.

Ten years ago, she got what she calls the best gift of life: her husband, who convinced her to have two babies, who are her motivation and inspiration. She is convinced that happiness is a choice, her choice, and that having a positive outlook and keeping your vision is essential to overcoming all challenges that life brings.

The same year that the company went through a restructure, she lost her father and got her feet burned on a family getaway. Talking with Masayo is so uplifting. She doesn't mention the two painful moments that were very important in shaping her, but that her positive outlook of life allowed her to keep moving forward. Through her story, you can see how her life compass guides her in every decision and movement she makes. Her values of courage, drive, compassion, and empathy are present in her day-to-day. What are your values and are you showing up to the world everyday true to them, true to yourself?

How Gratitude, Forgiveness, Compassion, and Love Impact Our Professional Career

> *"The best and most beautiful things in the world, cannot be seen or even heard, but must be felt with the heart."*
> **– Helen Keller**

Your life compass guides your decisions every day and shapes your journey, and resiliency helps you to face challenges and get richer outcomes from the lessons learned. Integrating the virtues of gratitude, forgiveness, compassion, and love takes you to a different level of transformation and evolution. We went through several spaces of our life to get to know ourselves better, but we wouldn't complete that journey without discussing how the virtues of gratitude, forgiveness, love, and compassion impact our careers. As holistic, multidimensional, human beings, those four virtues play an important role in our lives.

How we live them has an impact on how we experience life and how judgmental we are.

1. Gratitude: the act of appreciation.
2. Forgiveness: the act of stopping feeling angry or resentful toward (someone) for an offense, flaw, or mistake. It's a gift to ourselves, a process to clean our path and keep moving forward.
3. Compassion: sympathetic pity and concern for the suffering or misfortunes of others. The ability to understand and share the feelings of another.
4. Love: deep affection and appreciation for someone or something.

The four virtues together allow us to face challenges from a space of awareness and strengthen our resilience to bounce back from them. When you are aware of your unique value in life and you feel true love for yourself, you are in a better position to forgive yourself when you make mistakes and learn from them with gratitude and compassion, bouncing back and integrating the life lessons faster. This is not only for you, it is also so that you can see others with compassion, too. It allows you to be an example of change and create a positive environment where people around you can grow and thrive.

When I moved to Arizona last year, I got to connect with a person that showcases all of those virtues in her day-to-day. Her name is Andrea and I will share her story with you so you can identify how all those play together in creating a positive business environment, not only for her but for all of us that surround her.

She was born in Costa Rica and she was the first of her eight siblings to get to university. She recalls the importance of love by serving others, as her parents always taught her that we must do community service. It doesn't matter if you have or do not have economic resources, helping and serving others is a must. That learning and embedding compassion made her identify the needs of many of her classmates in the university, and she became president of the student's association, not to get power but to serve and create opportunities and make a difference for them. She shows up in gratitude, acknowledging that experience as an impactful one of growth, as she visited other countries in Central America and learned about the social differences and needs of many people. Not all of this was as easy as it sounds on paper—of course, she faced challenges, where the four virtues played an important role for her to keep moving forward with her vision to create a better world for herself and those around her. Of course, there were many moments when she was required to bring forgiveness to the table.

She started working as an engineer back in 2011 and got married 2013. In 2014 she had her first baby. When she was on maternity leave, she learned that her job was being impacted by her group closure, and she would have six months to find a new job. Her manager, who was a great sponsor for her, advocated for her to get a position in Arizona, and she got the position. She expressed that as a bittersweet moment, as many of her coworkers didn't have jobs. At that moment, her husband was finishing his career at the university, but decided to support her in this career opportunity. She was scared but took the opportunity, thinking that it would be a good example her family. Everything went very smoothly, without any roadblocks. They didn't have close family, but their church and faith became their root and provided them with the stability that they needed. She also recalls how important the Costa Rican community was in helping them to get settled. Andrea feels comfortable asking for help and at the same time is always ready to give a hand to whomever needs it. She volunteered herself to support the local Costa Rican network and nowadays is the lead that organizes all the network activities.

She highlights that she also got great support from her work core team and her boss. She describes her former boss as a visionary, who invited her to many activities at her house in order help her to connect with the local community. Her former boss was a great connector to her new networks.

Although she has always been in the same job, she constantly looks for different opportunities and has expanded her job. In 2016, she felt the call to feed her soul and engaged in the company diversity and inclusion activities. Her virtues of love, compassion, gratitude, and forgiveness always drive her to pay it forward, helping others to honor all the hands the have opened doors for her.

She had a difficult second pregnancy and refocused her priorities to take care of her baby, who needed more attention. He was born a month early and was diagnosed with Down syndrome. He opened new perspectives of life for her. He became that motor to inspire her to continue contributing to the company diversity and inclusion initiatives, creating opportunities for the diverse talent.

She states that the most important person in her life is her husband, who is a real partner. He has expanded her wings, looking for opportunities to support her. She believes that without his unconditional love and support she wouldn't be where she is in her career or in life as a mom and professional leader.

As you can see from Andrea's story, the love and service are present throughout her different spaces in life. Her gratitude to those that have given her a hand is translated into her giving a hand to those that surround her. Her compassionate view allows her to see things that others don't and to create opportunities for those that are in need. I am full of gratitude for her presence in my life, as she has opened doors and has followed the example of her boss, connecting me to many people. Her positive footprint on my transition from Costa Rica to Arizona has been very important in my career.

How are you using the virtues of love, compassion, forgiveness, and gratitude in your life?

My Resilience Commitment: Taking the Power Back

Write down how you commit to create a positive path for yourself and bring the help that you need to keep your journey moving onwards. How do you commit to take power back when roadblocks show up in your way? How do you continuously strengthen your resiliency, clarify your life compass, and embed the virtues of love, compassion, forgiveness, and gratitude in your life? Are you ready to make that commitment? Commitment is the foundation of great achievements.

An excerpt from *Walk the Talk*, by Eric Harvey and Steve Ventura:

> *"Commitment:*
>
> *Think of someone you know who is 'a person of good character.' Lock his or her image in your mind. Now take a moment to reflect on the things this person says and does… the personal characteristics that make him or her a role model for you. What comes to mind? What do you see?*
>
> *Chances are that high on the list of your role model's qualities is COMMITMENT—the unwavering dedication to being a good family member and friend… to doing his or her best at work and away from the job… to doing what's right, noble, and decent.*
>
> *Committed people like your role model just seem to have their heads and hearts in the right place. They keep their priorities straight. They stay focused on what's important. They know, inherently, that what they believe must drive how they behave—and how they behave ultimately determines the character they possess, the reputation they enjoy, and the legacy they leave."*

Abraham Lincoln said this about commitment:

> *"COMMITMENT is what transforms a promise into reality. It is the words that speak boldly of your intentions. And the actions which speak louder than the words.*

It is making the time when there is none. Coming through time after time after time, year after year after year. Commitment is the stuff character is made of; the power to change the face of things. It is the daily triumph of integrity over skepticism."

My commitment to myself:

I commit to keep myself grounded and connected to my core values of respect, courage, transparency, and collaboration. I acknowledge that I am connected to my journey fellows, as the aspen trees by our roots and essence. I am here to help and be helped. I commit to give back for and pay forward all the help that has been given to me.

I commit to have a compassionate look at those situations that take me out of my comfort zone. I will intentionally take myself out of my comfort zone to keep myself growing and learning. I purposefully create the conditions for gratitude, love, compassion, and forgiveness to arise and flow through me. I adapt and flourish in the face of change. I honor my ancestors and all their heritage by making the best use of the gifts that were given to me and contribute to my journey. I get conscious of my continuous improvement as the world needs the best version of me every day. I commit to make a difference in the world through my work, a work that matters. I commit to take care of my mental and physical health, performing activities that nourish my mind and body, such as daily meditation and pray practice, plus adopting healthy food choices and exercising every day.

I commit to continuously learn new things to enrich my presence on the planet. I commit to show appreciation and gratitude to my life fellow travelers. I commit to choose happiness over cynicism. When difficult situations come, I commit to feel the pain and move out of it as soon as possible. I commit to keep moving forward. I commit!

Chapter 10
PRACTICAL HACKS

*"Twenty years from now you will be more
disappointed by the things that you didn't do than
by the ones you did do. So throw off the bowlines.
Sail away from the safe harbor. Catch the trade
winds in your sails. Explore. Dream. Discover."*
– Mark Twain

Now that you released the best version of yourself, I want to share with you some of the tools that helped me keep track on my path of learning and growing and on that continuous journey of conquering myself.

You Time: Do What You Love and
Take Care of You and Your Bubble

What is not in your calendar or agenda doesn't exist, so go ahead and book special time for you. At least once a week, pick a special activity that you know is a gift from you to you. Sometimes I get asked, what can it be? Here is my personal list. Do yours and ensure you engage in at least one once a week:

- Pray
- Morning and night meditation
- Family time
- Reading
- Swimming in the ocean
- Scuba diving
- Wine tasting
- Time with friends
- Visiting a new place that connects me with nature
- Walking in the park
- Taking a new class
- Journaling
- Creating a new recipe
- Volunteering
- Weight lifting
- Yoga
- Dance

I call that sacred space that only the people who occupy a special place in my life can into "my bubble." We are all different and have different priorities in life. What works for me, might not necessarily work for others, and that is all good. As we say in Costa Rica: Pura Vida!

The people that I welcome to my bubble are those that don't lose their time criticizing others, because they focus their time on improving themselves and, if they have an observation about someone, they personally share it with that person face-to-face. I love problem solvers, those that are resourceful and always have a solution at hand.

The growth mindset people that expand you just with their presence, they don't have time to compare themselves with others, because they are always learning new things and involved in productive stuff.

They have a CAN-DO attitude. Nothing is perfect and we may not have the answers, but we will find a solution.

The heroes of their lives, not the victims, are those that show gratitude for life, that pave the way for others and ask for help.

I know that we all have different stories and each have a different journey, but we all have the same responsibility, which is to release the best version of ourselves to the world. To assume ownership and responsibility. To make a good investment of our time. I am a work in progress, but I know that life is too short, and I try to be selective about those that I let get in my bubble!

"The shoe that fits one person pinches another;
there is no recipe for living that suits all cases."
– Carl Jung

Meditation

We already talked about mindfulness and how important it is to be present and breathe in order to center ourselves, but I want to share about meditation as a technique that has helped me to manage stress and focus on my objectives and plans. I incorporated it into my life on a daily basis, and over the last two years I have done a morning and an evening practice. There are many types of meditation and you can pick which makes sense to you. A prayer is a form of meditation. I invite you to find a calm and peaceful place where you can disconnect from the world around you, including electronic devices, unless you decide to have a guided meditation on your iPad or cell phone. I like the guided ones as give me a sense of focus, but you can choose to just have five minutes of silencing your mind, no thoughts. If they come, tell them "No thank you" and return to silence. You get to identify what works for you.

Other Tips

1. Strengthen your emotional intelligence. Be conscious and aware of your behaviors and how you are impacting yourself and your surroundings. Anger, envy, and any other negative emotion is a charge of toxins for your body.

2. Implement curiosity versus judgment. When you catch yourself judging, change the thought for something positive.

3. Self-compassion and mindfulness are powerful tools to keep you evolving.

4. Look for new stuff to learn. Be strategic with your time. Every activity must be on your calendar. That way, you become more conscious about how you are investing your days. This gives you perspective.

5. When you don't feel comfortable with a situation, before reacting dig into yourself about the why. Is it maybe that the discomfort comes from your own paradigms?

6. There are many ways to see the world and many possible solutions. Your way is NOT the only way, nor the best way. Keep yourself humble and open.

7. Don't jump to conclusions quickly, nor to explanations. Always pause.

8. Silence can become your best friend. Get used to the spaces of silence as a way to have a clearer perspective of things.

9. Face your fears. They vanish when you confront them.

10. Don't put yourself or any other in a box, nor add labels. Respect and embrace the differences.

11. Whenever you get advice, test it and question yourself: is the other person projecting their fears on you? Of course they do, because they love you, but don't make decisions based on others fears.

12. Observe your thoughts and the words that come out of your mouth. Is it in alignment with your life vision?

13. Look at who surrounds you. That tells a lot about you.

14. Life brings infinite opportunities. Open yourself to receive the infinite gifts.

15. Pave the way for others.

16. You deserve the space that you are occupying. You earned it!

17. Don't be afraid of your own power.

18. Be appreciative. Don't forget from where you come and how you got there.

19. Family keeps you rooted.

20. I am just like you and you are just like me.

21. You don't need to be right, but you need to move forward.

CONCLUSION

I am so excited that you reached this point. Congratulations for taking ownership of your career and for not letting others make decisions on your behalf! That requires bravery and focus.

My call to action to you is that you fully engage with this process. Use it over and over and bring others along with you. We are here together on this journey and with the responsibility of sharing with others all those tools and practices that have allowed us to get where we are.

My wish is that you unleash your potential over and over, embracing this beautiful life in full, understanding and enjoying its beautiful moments, and when pain or challenges come, understanding that all will pass as the seasons and the days and nights, and that after every single challenge you won't be the same, but in the process, you will become stronger. I promise.

It's your responsibility to use the gifts that you get during those moments of happiness and challenges to become the light for many others and help them to pass that process that you already went through.

I would like to refresh all of the main concepts and all your commitments made during the seven weeks that it takes to complete this process. If you decide to make it shorter or longer, that's okay, just ensure that you complete all of the exercises and make the commitment to share this knowledge with at least two more women, so we all keep expanding our footprint of growth.

You learned that you are not alone. Many people face the same career challenges as you. Actually, I bet that you identified with some of the stories of the seven wonderful women who joined us on this book journey. I've been there, too. Facing challenge after challenge, but moving forward. The biggest strength comes from the inside, from your decision and bravery to keep moving. It could be imperfect, but what is important is to keep moving forward and onwards.

There are many processes out there. I picked and shared with you what has worked for me. I'll bet that you have many other processes or techniques that you can share to overcome challenges and have the career of your dreams. I would appreciate your sharing, not only with me, but with others, too.

Recall always that being aware is essential for our growth. Have clear what your core values and strengths are, and be conscious of those life agreements or contracts that are not serving you. It could be done, not by you but by any of your ancestors, be aware, question them.

Honor your ancestors as you are here because of all of their history, but remember that you are the owner of your life and the only person responsible for defining your vision and building your meaningful career. Ensure you control your schedule to serve your purpose.

You designed the career of your dreams. What is the commitment stamped in your career manifesto? Frame it and have it close to you. You acknowledged your career cycles and defined who you want in your journey and who would add value, too. Did you already engage those new potential contributors to your career? You defined your objectives for 1/5/10 and defined who your current board of advisors, BOA, is. Purposefully identify the ones that you need on your BOA to advance faster towards the career of your dreams.

How are you leveraging the value of service in your career journey?

Let's bring to the table your values, strengths, hobbies, and how you ignited the process to build the best version of yourself.

Resilience plays an important role in our journey, and I hope that you have developed that muscle and continue to strengthen it.

My wish is that all of the tips helped you to ensure that you are your top priority. As Donovan Livingston, Harvard graduate, stated in his commencement speech in 2016, "Together we can inspire galaxies for generations to come. No, no, 'sky is not the limit' is just the beginning. Lift off!"

Acknowledgements

It is said that it takes a village to raise a kid, and it took me a village to complete this book. This is a book that consolidates more than twenty years of working experience, but it is far beyond working experience. We are holistic humans and how we show up in the world is a reflection of all of our roles and interactions. One of the historic leaders that I admire a lot is Gandhi, and one of his quotes that really inspires me is this: "Happiness is when what you think, what you say, and what you do are in harmony." Life is too short to think that we can live life in pieces and that we can disconnect those pieces and show up happy every day. So, I want to thank you, all my travel fellows, all those people that have touched my life, not just at work, but since I landed into this earth.

I landed in a difficult situation, My mom didn't have an easy process for my birth, but what it's certain is that my birth was surrounded by unconditional love. That's why I want to thank you, my grandparents, who are no longer physically with me but eternally in my heart. Their footprints are those endless echoes of pure love. From grandpa Carlos (Chino Alvarado), I recall my dinners alone with him, dancing on his feet, the secret place for candies. Grandma Leti, we spent many more years together, the most beautiful dresses, our trips together, lunches and dinners full of savvy and advice. Grandma Luz, a very different relationship but definitely her bravery, strength, the rosary, my first make up and her red lipstick are memories that I treasure. I didn't meet grandpa Humberto, but his entrepreneurship footprint is very present on my son Andres. Uncles, aunts and more than one hundred cousins were part of my fun and happy childhood. But there are three very special aunts that have been always very present: tia Ofe, with her daily prayer and countless candles lighted to support my journey; my aunt Mimi, the one that every single morning sends me a positive message for the day, always very accurate to what I need. Aunt Vicky, the one that was single when I was a little kid and took care of me, and I still remember playing with her and aunt Mimi, "ambo ambo matarilerilero." Amazing, the flow of love from my family during my childhood and adulthood.

We are part of the working class and my parents an amazing example of effort and commitment, an example to always deliver the best.

Mom, my hero, she gave me wings and called me her star: "The sky is not the limit, it's just the beginning." She supported all my dreams; the dream could be crazy, but she would always be there for me. She even paid for an English class where I learned while sleeping. Yes, I learned English while sleeping! It wasn't perfect, but it has helped me to communicate.

Dad, always working hard to give us the best, keeping us always grounded. I am so glad he retired, because those have been the best years, where we have been able to enjoy them fully. We have created amazing memories and he has built very close bonding with my son, nephew, and niece. Just one example: mom and dad flew to support my son while I was on business travels and sat next to me endless hours while I was writing.

My main BOA pusher and inspirer, my son Andres. There was no week that you didn't check on me to see how I was advancing and how many words were written that week. You started my Facebook page for the book, you support me and inspire me to be a better human every single day. You just rock Andy, my motor and inspiration. You are by far the best gift that I got from God in life.

My brother Charlie and sister Nina, more unconditional love in my life. Both of them have been essential in my growth and support. Nina took care of my son while she was in university (attending at night) and I was working, which gave me the peace of mind required to thrive at work. She got married to Harold, who has been another unconditional brother in my life. Charlie, the best designer ever, and always fully supportive to whatever Andy or I need. The cover of this book is a co-design with my dad, and all of the beautiful charts inside the book were created by Charlie. He got married to one of the engineers that I most admire, Marce. She was my friend before I introduced them, and is now my friend and sister.

My nephew Gabriel, as his name meaning states … he is a messenger, a messenger of unconditional love to our lives. My little and powerful Nana, this girl that at just three years old, when I tried to get her into a pair of princess pajamas told me no, I want superhero pajamas. She is convinced that she will save Hulk. She is my superhero and inspiration, along with Sara, our youngest baby girl in the family, plus all of the other family girls and boys. I am so looking forward to seeing what life brings to us.

As you can see, family has determined and strengthen my path, but in the journey, there have been many important fellows that have contributed to this book:

The seven women: those wonderful women that jumped into my call when I requested a summary of their journeys, as I knew it would serve as example to you, my loved reader. Thank you Angie, Andrea, Erika, Fernanda, Masayo, Natalia, and Shirlene, for opening your hearts and lives to others, embracing vulnerability to share your struggles and share how you overcame them.

My friend and guide, Perla. Thank you for so many years of being with me in the most difficult times, showing me the way to be peace in the middle of the storm and to keep moving forward. Thank you for opening paths to me that I didn't even imagine that I could walk.

My spiritual team: Sylvia and Johnattan, Vivi, Nosara, Alejandro, Memo and Hellen.

My Ticas sisters in Arizona: Fanny, Ana, Ana Cristina, Aracelly, Syl, Maryanela, Katti and Carito.

My ticos brothers in Arizona: Javi, Pepe, Jose, Tavo, Miguel, Cesar and Marte … thank you for embracing Andy in your cycling team. This is so meaningful and important for us.

My IEM family: Machita and Ale, Mari and Montgo, Eu and Carlos, Gaby and Rafa, Gaby Ch. and Memo, Yeya and Luis, Anita and Manfred, plus your parents and all the kids. The years keep going and our ties keep growing strong.

My Aspen Institute and CALI fellows. You all have always been there for me, willing to help when I need you. Special thanks to my big brothers and sisters: Arturo and Leo, Luigi and Alex. Alexandra, you have been my mentor and guide.

To all the individuals that have led and inspired me, even those that I watched from afar. To those that I have had the privilege to lead. To my peers. Thank you all for the experiences shared.

Special thanks to Roz, for the life-changing opportunities. You opened doors, created spaces, and gave voice to underrepresented minorities and paved the way for many of us. Thank you for the opportunities that you and Pia gave me.

Thank you Shelly for your trust and for letting me witness how female leadership can make a big change in people's lives, bringing to the table aspects unseen by our male fellows. Thank you for sharing the Suite of Advisors, which I translated in this book as Board of Advisors. Diana, thank you for your savvy, open, and direct feedback that helped me grow. Thank you Marcelino, Nuno, Jaime, Gabriela (the two Gabrielas), Francisco, Memo, don Alvaro and don Gerardo, for being part of my growth and journey. A special thank you to my mentors:

Bob, Mike, Mohsen, Vince, Barb, Suzanne, Tim, and Cin, for your trust and open conversations.

Martha, Laura, Carol, Mayi, Milena, Noemy, Margarita, Andrea, Misha, Ileana, Adri, Jenn, and Alba, thank you for making the difference and being my advocates.

To the Morgan James Publishing team: Special thanks to David Hancock, CEO & Founder for believing in me and my message. To my Author Relations Manager, Margo Toulouse, thanks for making the process seamless and easy. Many more thanks to everyone else, but especially Jim Howard, Bethany Marshall, and Nickcole Watkins.

Last but not least, thank you Angela Lauria for the wonderful process you created. I couldn't believe that this would be possible in nine weeks. Your process really works! It's an honor to work with you, Cheyenne, Ora, Bethany, and the rest of the team, plus sharing experiences with all of the authors that are engaged in this journey of creating a positive footprint on the planet.

About the Author

Karla Blanco is a corporate leader with more than twenty years' experience working in a Fortune 100 corporation. She studied customs administration and holds an MBA with an international business emphasis.

She is an Aspen Fellow from the Central America Leaders Initiative (CALI), from the program of Leadership to Significance. She is also a certified mentor with Vital Voices in Costa Rica, mentoring entrepreneurs and working on efforts to engage women in science and technology and to raise consciousness about the importance of educating girls and women to drive economic improvement. Due to her effort and leadership, the Vital Voices Costa Rican chapter launched its first group of male mentors at a global level to support diversity and inclusion.

She has gone through many restructuring processes and layouts throughout her career. Her positive outlook on life and ownership of her growth process has allowed her to have a meaningful career and has helped her mentees to unlock their potential to enjoy meaningful careers and fulfilling lives by unleashing the best version of themselves. In 2009 she was recognized by Costa Rican business newspaper *El Financiero* as one of the top 40 country leaders under 40 years old.

Karla enjoys spending time with her son, Andres, her friends, and her family. She has a special passion for the ocean and is a certified scuba diver. Meditation is part of her daily routine and she also enjoys reading and dancing.

Thank You!

Thanks for reading my book, *Unleash Your Career Potential: 7 Steps to Living Your Dream.*

The fact that you've gotten to this point in the book tells me something important about you: you are ready for a different outcome in your journey, you are ready to design your future and enjoy the career of your dreams.

To support your journey, I created a special gift just for you. Send me an email at KarlaUYP@gmail.com to claim your free workbook.

Sincerely,

Karla Blanco

Author of *Unleash Your Career Potential*